Basic Chemistry Questions for GCSE

National Curriculum Edition

Bernard Abrams
MA CChem MRSC FRAS

ADT College, London

Stanley Thornes (Publishers) Ltd

First published in 1994 by
Stanley Thornes (Publishers) Ltd
Ellenborough House
Wellington Street
CHELTENHAM GL50 1YD
England

Reprinted 1995

A catalogue record for this book is available from the British Library.

ISBN 0 7487 1725 0

Typeset by Tech-Set, Gateshead, Tyne & Wear.
Printed and bound in Great Britain at Redwood Books, Trowbridge, Wiltshire.

Contents

Preface to the National Curriculum Edition

Chemical science surrounds us at all times, yet pupils can remain unaware of the relevance of the subject and often find tests and examinations difficult as a result. By using a wide variety of question styles and contexts, I hope that pupils will gain confidence as well as knowledge and understanding by working through the questions.

The pressures on a teacher's time are considerable and increasing. There is a constant demand for exercises that are effective, stimulating and also relatively easy to correct and evaluate.

This book has been written and more recently revised to help reinforce a basic understanding of Chemical science in both double award at GCSE and Science: Chemistry within the framework of the National Curriculum.

The specific aims of this question book are as follows:
1. To provide a framework within which pupils can compile a useful set of correct notes by working through and completing the various assignments, either on their own or with the help of the teacher.
2. To develop a pupil-centred approach to learning.
3. To provide an opportunity to develop pupil skills in numeracy and literacy.
4. To provide stimulating and varied material which can reinforce and consolidate the basic chemical facts needed for Key Stage 4, whether in tests or in homework or classwork assignments. It can also, of course, be used as a revision programme.
5. To provide material that can be useful to students independently studying chemistry.
6. To develop scientific skills such as observation, measurement, interpretation and application.
7. To provide graded material that can be used in a mixed-ability or streamed class, so that all pupils will achieve some degree of success.
8. To provide material that is easy to use, easy to mark, and can be used in a wide variety of different ways by the teacher.

This National Curriculum edition contains up-to-date material relating to all the major areas of chemistry. It also includes a selection of questions specific to various extension topics.

Anticipating the difficulty some pupils may have with diagrams, I have simplified many of those essential to syllabuses. Although there are questions asking pupils to copy diagrams I expect that in many cases they will be traced.

Bernard Abrams,
ADT College, London, 1994

Acknowledgements

The author and publisher are grateful to Ian Ward and Pan Books for permission to use the extracts on pp. 153 and 158, and to the following for permission to reproduce examination questions:

London East Anglian Group
Midland Examining Group
Northern Examining Association
Southern Examining Group
Welsh Joint Education Committee

   Many people have helped in the production of this book, and I would like to thank colleagues for their constructive criticisms of the questions. Finally it is my pleasure to thank the publishers Stanley Thornes, and all those involved in the design and production of this book.

   Every effort has been made to contact copyright holders, and I apologise to any I have not been able to reach.

Theme 1

Matter and Particles

1 STATES OF MATTER

Solids, Liquids and Gases

1

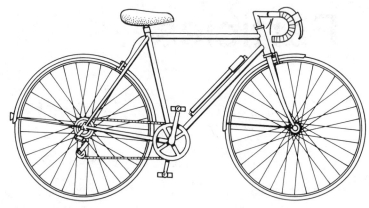

The diagram shows a pedal cycle.

Explain why

a)   the frame is made from steel, a solid.

b)   a liquid, oil, is used to lubricate the chain.

c)   the tyres are filled with air, a gas.

2   This packet of sugar claims that it is 'quick dissolving':

a)   What is likely to be different about the sugar in the packet, compared to ordinary sugar, which makes it quick dissolving?

b)   Design an experiment to test whether or not the sugar does dissolve quicker than ordinary sugar. List the apparatus you would use, what you would do, and how you would make sure the comparison was fair.

3   You have been given the following equipment:

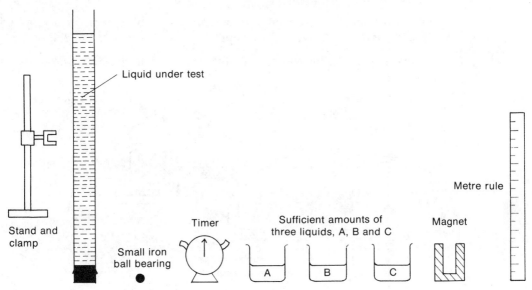

Liquid under test

Stand and clamp

Metre rule

Timer

Sufficient amounts of three liquids, A, B and C

Magnet

Small iron ball bearing

A   B   C

1.5 m length of hollow glass tube

Describe how you would all use the equipment to measure the viscosity (resistance to flow) of the three liquids. Give an outline of the method you would use and the measurements you would take. How would you place the liquids in order of increasing viscosity using your results?

4   Two plastic syringes are joined by a length of hollow rubber tubing. One is empty, the other contains a liquid which also fills the connecting tube. A house brick rests against the plunger of the empty syringe as shown.

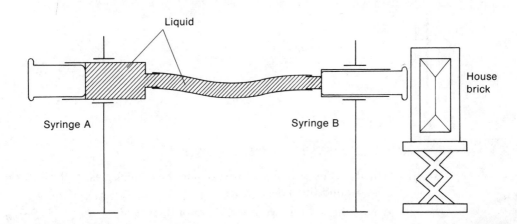

Liquid

Syringe A

Syringe B

House brick

a) i) What will happen when the plunger of syringe A is pushed in?
   ii) Why does this happen?

b) The syringes and tubing are emptied and dried, and the experiment is repeated with air in syringe A. What will happen?

c) Use the diagram below to explain why a gas bubble in a car's brake fluid is dangerous.

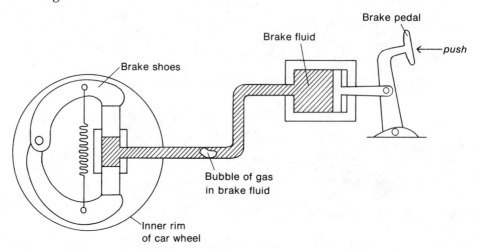

5   The diagram shows an alcohol thermometer, which uses an ethanol–dye mixture to indicate the temperature. Data on ethanol (and mercury, another liquid commonly used in thermometers) is given in the table.

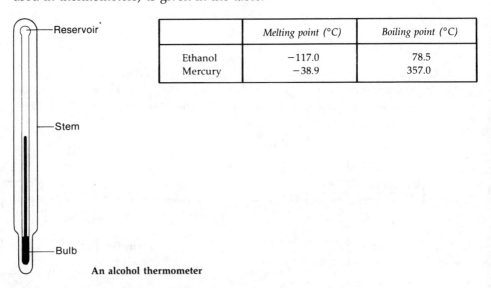

	Melting point (°C)	Boiling point (°C)
Ethanol	−117.0	78.5
Mercury	−38.9	357.0

An alcohol thermometer

a) i) Why does the bulb of the thermometer have thick glass at the base but thin glass around the sides?
   ii) Why is there a reservoir at the top of the stem?

b)   Copy and complete the following table by listing one advantage and one disadvantage of each liquid for use in a thermometer.

	Advantage	Disadvantage
Ethanol Mercury		

c)   The liquid in the alcohol thermometer freezes at $-118.5\,°C$. Comment on this in view of the melting point of ethanol given.

6   The boiling point of a liquid increases as the external pressure increases. Use this information to explain the following observations.

a)   If a cup of water is placed in an air-tight container and the air is removed using a vacuum pump, the water will boil without being heated.

b)   Food cooks more quickly in a pressure cooker.

c)   The accurately measured boiling point of a sample of pure water may change from one day to the next if there is an accompanying change in the weather.

d)   It is dangerous to remove the radiator cap when a car's water cooling system is overheating.

7   Two gas cylinders have been found. One is known to contain a poisonous gas under pressure, the other a partial vacuum, but they are identical in all other respects. In principle, would it be possible to identify the poison gas cylinder by weighing them?

Explain your answer.

8   Three rigid, hollow metal containers have tubes connected to beakers of water as shown in the diagram. All three contain air and are identical except for their internal conditions.

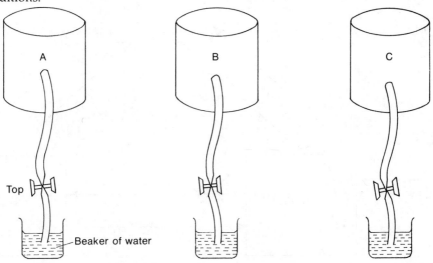

When the taps are opened, the following results are noted:

Container	Observations
A	The water level in the beaker drops
B	Nothing happens
C	Bubbles appear at the end of the tube

What can you deduce from these observations about the conditions inside each container before the taps were opened?

9   a)   A partly inflated balloon is placed inside a glass container, which is then evacuated. As the air is pumped out of the container what will happen to

   i)   the number of molecules in the balloon?

   ii)   the volume of the balloon?

   b)   Explain why weather balloons, designed to fly at high altitude, are only partly inflated at launch.

Changes of State

1   Copy and complete the diagram below by adding the *reverse process* for each of those labelled.

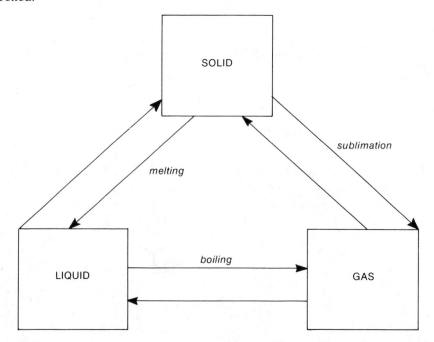

2 a) Use the data on the ten substances below to produce a table, which shows the state of each substance at room temperature (25 °C).

Substance	Melting point (°C)	Boiling point (°C)
Selenium	217	685
Anisole	−38	154
Beryllium	1280	2477
Bromine	−7	59
Propane	−188	−42
Benzamide	132	290
Cobalt	1492	2900
Radon	−71	−62
Anthracene	216	340
Propyne	−103	−23

Solids	Liquids	Gases

b) List the substances in order of increasing boiling point.

c) Which substance is a liquid over the smallest range of temperature?

d) Which of the substances is gaseous at −50 °C?

e) Which substance has the lowest freezing point?

f) Which substance is a liquid at 2500 °C?

3 A substance melts at 92 °C and boils at 190 °C. The arrangement of particles in the substance at 50 °C and 250 °C are shown below.

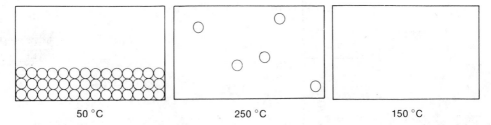

50 °C   250 °C   150 °C

a) Copy the diagram, with labels, and draw in the arrangement of particles you would expect at 150 °C.

b) At which of the three temperatures is the motion of the particles limited to vibration?

c) When the temperature of 10 g of the substance changes from 50 °C to 60 °C, state whether each of the following quantities increases, decreases, or stays the same:

i)   the number of particles present

ii) the average energy of the particles

iii) the density of the substance

4   The diagrams on the left below show what happens to an ice cube as it is heated
using a Bunsen burner. The diagrams on the right show what happens to the
particles (molecules) during heating, but the order has been changed.

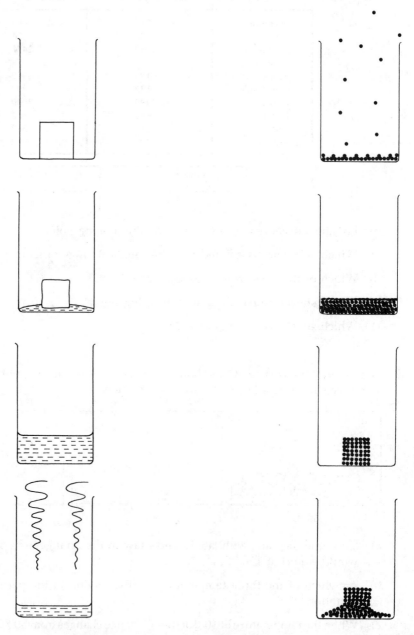

a)   i)   Copy the ice diagrams in the same sequence.

ii)   Draw the correct model next to each ice diagram.

b)   As the liquid water changes to water vapour, the temperature remains constant.
Explain what happens to the energy provided by the Bunsen burner.

5 Explain the following:

a) When surgical spirit evaporates on your skin the area becomes cold.

b) A burn from steam at 100 °C is worse than a burn from water at 100 °C.

c) Panting helps dogs to cool down in hot weather.

6 The following diagrams represent the arrangement of particles in a solid, a liquid and a gas:

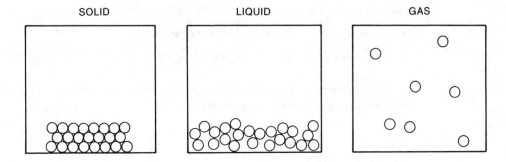

a) Referring to the diagrams, explain why gases can be compressed easily but solids and liquids cannot.

b) Why does a bicycle with air-filled rubber tyres give a smoother ride than one with solid rubber tyres?

7 A sample of ice was taken out of a freezer at −10 °C and left in a container in the kitchen. The temperature was taken every 2 minutes, until no further change took place. The temperature in the kitchen was 21 °C.

a) Sketch the graph you would expect to obtain if temperature (y-axis) was plotted against time (x-axis) for the results of this experiment. Add labels to show the melting point of ice and room temperature.

b) i) Mark a point 'X' on your graph where the kinetic energy of the water molecules is increasing.

ii) Mark a point 'Y' on your graph where the potential energy of the water molecules is increasing.

iii) Mark a different point 'Z' on your graph where the molecules are capable of vibrational movement only.

2   MIXTURES AND SEPARATION

1   Copy and complete the following sentences to show how you would separate the
two substances in each mixture:

a)   Sand and water can be separated by . . .

b)   Iron filings and copper filings can be separated by . . .

c)   Oil and water can be separated by . . .

d)   Sand and sodium chloride (common salt) can be separated by . . .

e)   Water and ethanol (alcohol) can be separated by . . .

f)   A mixture of blue and red inks can be separated by . . .

2   a)   Copy the diagram of the apparatus used to carry out fractional distillation of
crude oil in the laboratory. Add labels at the positions indicated.

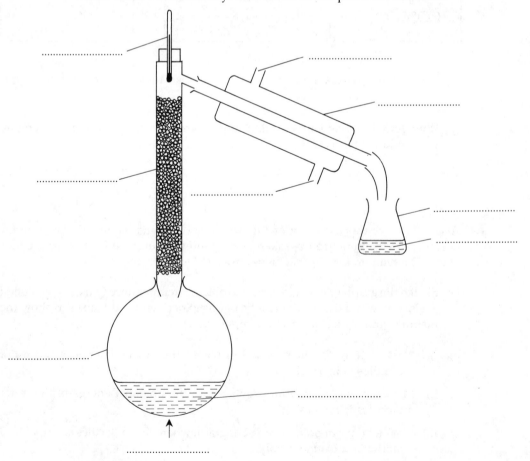

b) The following table gives details of some fractions collected during the distillation of crude oil.

Fraction	Boiling point range/°C	Colour
1	160–190	Yellow
2	200–230	Orange
3	240–270	Brown

i) Is each fraction a pure compound? Explain your answer.

ii) Which fraction would be least viscous (most runny)?

iii) Which fraction would be most difficult to ignite, and would burn with the smokiest flame?

c) How does the apparatus separate crude oil into fractions? Give as much detail in your answer as you can.

d) Which of the following could be separated using fractional distillation?

    A.   Liquids which mix and which have different melting points

    B.   Liquids which mix and which have different boiling points

    C.   Liquids with very similar boiling points which do not mix

    D.   Liquids which mix, regardless of their melting or boiling points

    E.   Liquids with very similar melting points which do not mix

3 Ink is taken from the signature of a forged cheque and compared with the ink from the pens of 3 suspects (A, B and C) using paper chromatography. The result is shown below:

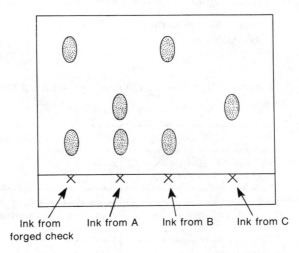

a) How could a sample of ink be taken from the forged cheque?

b) Describe how the chromatography experiment was carried out.

c) Which suspects could not be guilty?

4 The diagram below shows an unmanned rocket moving through space. The rocket uses liquid hydrogen and oxygen as its propellant.

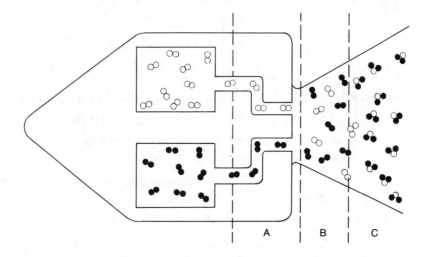

a) In which of the regions, A, B or C, is there

    i)   a compound?

    ii)   two elements in a pure state?

    iii)   a mixture of two elements?

b) Name the compound produced when hydrogen and oxygen react together.

c) Which of the following methods could be used to obtain hydrogen and oxygen from the compound produced when these elements react together?

      fractional distillation   **chromatography**   **electrolysis**
      crystallisation

5 Copy and complete the following table, which lists the differences between mixtures and compounds.

Mixtures	Compounds
No energy exchange with surroundings on formation.	
	Constituent elements can be recovered only by further reaction or electrolysis.
Mixtures can have any composition.	
	The properties of a compound rarely resemble those of its constituents.

6 a) In a colloidal system, what is the equivalent of

    i) the solvent in a solution

    ii) the solute in a solution?

b) Describe how you would use a light beam to decide whether a detergent powder forms a solution or a sol when added to water.

c) An iron(III) hydroxide sol can be prepared by adding a small volume of concentrated iron(III) chloride solution to a large excess of boiling water in a beaker. The process also produces some hydrochloric acid.

$$FeCl_3 \quad\quad + 3\,H_2O \longrightarrow Fe(OH)_3 \quad + 3\,HCl$$

FeCl$_3$	+ 3 H$_2$O	Fe(OH)$_3$	+ 3 HCl
concentrated solution	boiling water	iron(III) hydroxide sol	hydrochloric acid

The sol can be purified by dialysis. A simple dialyser can be made as shown in the diagram.

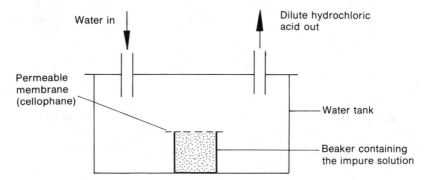

i) How could you show that the liquid leaving the dialyser was dilute hydrochloric acid and not pure water?

ii) Explain why hydrochloric acid was present in the liquid leaving the dialyser, while the iron(III) hydroxide was not.

iii) Give one important application of dialysis, and name the colloidal system involved.

3 ELEMENTS AND COMPOUNDS

Elements and Chemical Change

1 From the symbols shown, choose the correct symbol for each of the following elements.

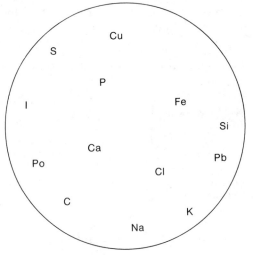

a) iron   b) sodium   c) chlorine   d) copper

e) potassium   f) carbon   g) lead   h) silicon

2 A student carried out the following experiment to investigate the effect of heat on a mixture of iron and sulphur. After heating for a few minutes, the mixture began to glow brightly. The glow spread through the contents of the tube after heating was stopped. When the tube had cooled the contents were tipped out onto a heat resistant bench mat. A grey solid had been formed.

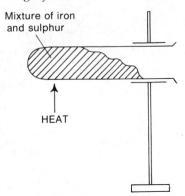

Mixture of iron and sulphur

HEAT

a) Suggest two methods for separating the iron and sulphur in the original mixture.

b) Write down two pieces of information from the description of the experiment which suggest that a chemical reaction has taken place.

c) Name the compound formed in the reaction.

d) Which of the following methods could be used to separate the iron and sulphur in the compound?

   magnetism   distillation   electrolysis   reaction with dilute acid

3

The diagrams above represents the arrangements of particles in eight different substances at room temperature. Which of the substances A–H

a) is a solid?

b) are liquids?

c) are gases?

d) are elements?

e) are compounds?

f) is a mixture?

g) could be water (H_2O)?

h) could be iron (Fe)?

i) could be hydrogen (H_2)?

j) could be iodine (I_2)?

k) could be helium (He)?

l) could be hydrogen chloride gas (HCl)?

m) could be a mixture of nitrogen and oxygen?

Metals and Non-metals

1 Copy and complete the following table, which compares the properties of metals and non-metals.

Metallic elements	Non-metallic elements
Conduct electricity Good conductors of heat	
	Brittle
Lustrous (shiny) Usually form positive ions	
	Oxides are generally acidic in solution

2 a) The following table lists the properties of five elements. The letters used are not the symbols for the elements.

Element	Solubility in water	Melting point (°C)	Electrical conductivity (solid)	Thermal conductivity
A	Reacts	39	Good	Good
B	Soluble	−101	Does not conduct	Poor
C	Insoluble	113	Does not conduct	Poor
D	Insoluble	−39	Good	Good
E	Insoluble	−157	Does not conduct	Poor

   i)   Which of the elements are metals?

   ii) Which of the non-metals are gaseous at room temperature (25 °C)?

   iii) Which of the elements is mercury?

   iv) Give two differences between metals and non-metals other than those mentioned in the table.

   b) i)   Which non-metallic element conducts electricity?

       ii) Name one semi-metal (metalloid).

3 a) Give the meaning of the terms **malleable** and **ductile**.

   b) Explain the following observations by referring to the structure of the solids involved:

       i)   Metals are good conductors of electricity as solids.

       ii) Metals are malleable and ductile while ionic solids are brittle.

   c) You have prepared a sample of a new alloy based on iron, and want to compare its resistance to corrosion with that of pure iron. Describe the tests you would carry out on the two samples, listing any chemicals and apparatus needed, and say how you would interpret the results. Explain how you would ensure that the comparison was a fair one.

4 THE PERIODIC TABLE

The Chemistry of Groups

1 Copy and complete the table below, which compares the characteristics of the alkali metals and transition metals.

Alkali metals	Transition metals
Soft, low density metals	
	React slowly with water or not at all
Form colourless compounds	
	Form more than one compound with chlorine and other elements (variable valency)
	Metals and their compounds often useful as redox catalysts

2 The boiling points of the first four elements in group 7 of the Periodic Table (the halogens) are given in the table below. The value for bromine has been left out.

Element	Boiling point (°C)
Fluorine	−188
Chlorine	−101
Bromine	
Iodine	+184

a) Write down the chemical symbol of each element in the order shown.

b) Name one halogen which is a gas at room temperature (25 °C)

c) i) Write down an estimate for the boiling point of bromine. Explain how you arrived at your answer.

   ii) Bromine is toxic. Draw a diagram of the apparatus you would use to test your prediction for the boiling point of bromine. Where would you carry out the experiment, and what precautions would you take?

3 Copy and complete the following sentences by choosing the correct word from the brackets.

a) The alkali metals are (soft/hard) and react (slowly/violently) with water.

b) Transition metals form many (coloured/colourless) compounds and have (high/low) densities.

c) Chlorine, a member of the (inert gases/halogens), forms a simple (positive/negative) ion.

d) Helium has (one/two) atoms in its molecules and reacts with (no/many) other elements.

e) Carbon is a (metallic/non-metallic) element which (conducts/does not conduct) electricity.

4 Carbon, silicon and germanium are three of the elements in group 4 of the Periodic Table. Group 4 is listed below.

C
Si
Ge
Sn
Pb

Some information on carbon and its compounds is given below:

Element	Density (g/cm^3)	Formula of chloride	Formula of oxide
Carbon	2.3	CCl_4	CO_2

a) Which elements are represented by the symbols Sn and Pb?

b) Name one element in group 4 which is

i) a metal   ii) a semi-metal (metalloid)   iii) a non-metal

c) Predict the formulae of the following compounds:

i) silicon chloride   ii) germanium oxide

d) The density of germanium is 5.4 g/cm^3. Estimate the density of silicon, showing how you arrived at your answer.

e) Describe one use of any *two* elements in group 4.

Periodicity

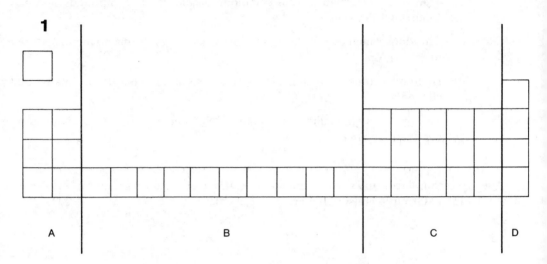

A portion of the Periodic Table is divided into 4 parts as shown. In which part (A–D) would you find:

a)   a metal which reacts violently with cold water?

b)   an element which doesn't form any compounds?

c)   a metal which has many coloured compounds?

d)   the element chlorine?

e)   a non-metal which conducts electricity?

f)   a gas which reacts with oxygen to form water?

g)   the metal with the highest melting point?

h)   an element X which forms an oxide X_2O_3?

2 In the Periodic Table shown below, the letters used are not the symbols of the elements. Choose the letter corresponding to an element which:

a) forms a hydroxide which is strongly alkaline.

b) forms a gaseous, acidic oxide in which atoms of the element and oxygen are in the ratio 1:2.

c) has atomic number 14.

d) has electron arrangement 2, 8, 7.

e) readily forms an ion carrying the charge -2.

f) forms more than one chloride.

g) has similar chemical properties to L.

h) is a non-metal which conducts electricity.

i) has the largest relative atomic mass.

j) readily forms an ion which has the same electron arrangement as X.

3 Some of the following statements concerning the Periodic Table are true, others are false. Copy them out, correcting any that are false.

a) In the Periodic Table, each row is called a period.

b) Elements in the same group have similar chemical properties.

c) There are more non-metals than metals in the Periodic Table.

d) In moving from left to right across the Periodic Table, elements become more metallic.

e) Elements in group 2 are called the halogens.

f) The alkali metals become more reactive as the group is descended.

g) The Periodic Table arranges the elements in order of increasing boiling point.

5 PARTICLES

Atoms, Molecules and Ions

1 All matter contains invisibly small particles. Explain each of the following situations by discussing the behaviour of these particles.

  a) Small pieces of smoke, which appear as bright dots in a smoke cell viewed under a microscope, jiggle about a lot as they move.

  b) Bromine vapour takes several minutes to diffuse through a container full of air, yet fills the container in a fraction of a second if the container has been evacuated beforehand.

  c) A balloon inflates when air is pumped inside.

  d) If a tin can with a tight-fitting lid is heated, the lid suddenly shoots off at high speed.

  e) A metal rod expands when heated.

2 The statement 'two oxygen molecules' can be written using symbols as $2O_2$. Copy and complete the following table by adding the missing statements or symbols.

Statement	Symbols
Two oxygen atoms	
	$4H_2O$
One hydrogen molecule	
	$3Cl^-$
Two ammonia molecules	
Three oxide ions	
	$2H_2O + O_2$
A chlorine atom and a hydrogen molecule	

3 The diagram below is a simple representation of a helium atom. The electric charge on each particle present is shown.

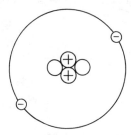

a) Copy the diagram and correctly label each of the following: nucleus, proton, neutron, electron.

b) What is the total charge of

   i)   the nucleus
   ii) the whole atom?

c) Copy and complete the sentence below to compare the masses of protons, neutrons and electrons.

   _____ and _____ are roughly _____ in mass, each being about 1800 times _____ than an _____.

d) Explain what is meant by

   i)   atomic number
   ii) mass number.

4 Details of the composition of five particles are given in the table.

Particle	Number of protons	Number of neutrons	Number of electrons
A	6	8	8
B	8	8	6
C	6	6	8
D	8	6	6
E	6	8	6

a) Which of the particles is a neutral atom?

b) Which particles are positive ions?

c) Which particles are ions carrying a charge of −2?

d) Which particle has the greatest mass?

e) Which particle is an isotope of E?

5   The diagram below shows some details of the structure of a lithium atom.

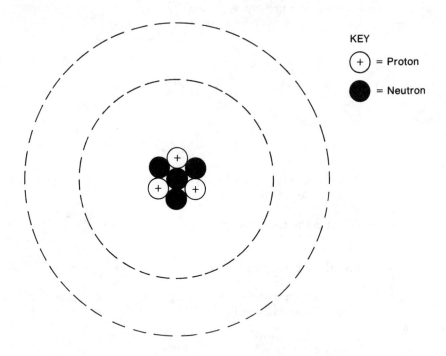

KEY

$(+)$ = Proton

● = Neutron

a) i)   Copy the diagram.

      ii) Complete it by drawing in the correct number of electrons in each shell. Use the symbol ⊖ to represent an electron.

b) What change occurs when the lithium atom becomes an ion?

Formulae

1   The structural formula of dichloromethane, a solvent used to remove caffeine from coffee, is shown below.

a) How many atoms are there in one molecule of dichloromethane?

b) What is the molecular formula of dichloromethane?

2   Copy and complete the table below:

	Structural formula	Molecular formula

a)    H — Cl

b)

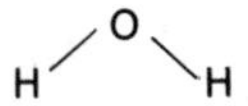

c)

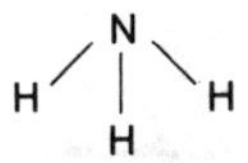

d)

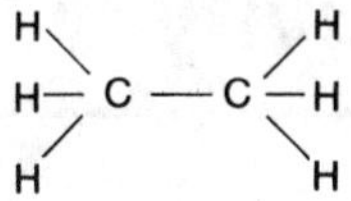

e)

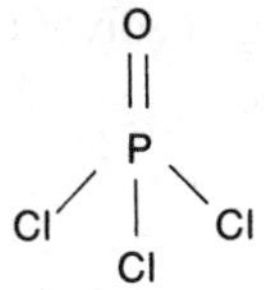

3   How many atoms are there in one molecule of each of the following compounds?

a)   ammonia, NH_3

b)   sulphuric acid, H_2SO_4

c)   glucose, $C_6H_{12}O_6$

d)   trinitrotoluene (TNT), $C_7H_5(NO_2)_3$

4   Ionic compounds are neutral overall. Copy the table of ion charges given below and use it to predict the formula of each compound a)–j).

Ion charge	+3	+2	+1	−1	−2
Ions	Aluminium Al^{3+}	Magnesium Mg^{2+}	Sodium Na^+	Chloride Cl^-	Oxide O^{2-}
		Calcium Ca^{2+}	Silver Ag^+	Hydroxide OH^-	Sulphate SO_4^{2-}
		Zinc Zn^{2+}	Ammonium NH_4^+	Nitrate NO_3^-	Carbonate CO_3^{2-}

a)   sodium chloride

b)   calcium oxide

c)   aluminium oxide

    d)   silver nitrate

    e)   zinc sulphate

    f)   magnesium hydroxide

    g)   calcium nitrate

    h)   sodium carbonate

    i)   ammonium sulphate

    j)   aluminium hydroxide

Atomic Structure and Reactivity

1 Sodium chloride (NaCl) is a solid with a high melting point. Carbon tetrachloride (CCl_4) is a volatile liquid which is used in industry as a solvent.

    a)   In which group of the periodic table is

        i)   sodium?

        ii) carbon?

    b)   The arrangement of electrons in a carbon atom may be written as 2, 4. Using this notation, write down the arrangement of electrons in an atom of

        i)   sodium

        ii) chlorine

    c)   Draw diagrams to show the electron arrangement in sodium chloride and in carbon tetrachloride. The outer shells only should be shown in each case.

2 a) Copy and complete the diagrams below to show the arrangement of electrons in atoms of hydrogen, carbon and chlorine.

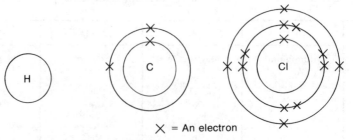

X = An electron

      (Atomic numbers: H = 1, C = 6, Cl = 17)

    b) i)   Draw a diagram to show the number of electrons in the outer shell of the carbon and chlorine atoms in a C–Cl bond in trichloromethane, $CHCl_3$.

        ii) Which inert gas has the same electron arrangement as the chlorine in trichloromethane?

3   An important use of sodium metal is in a nuclear power station, as shown below. The sodium absorbs the heat produced in the nuclear reactor. The hot sodium is then used to convert water into steam. The steam then drives the turbines.

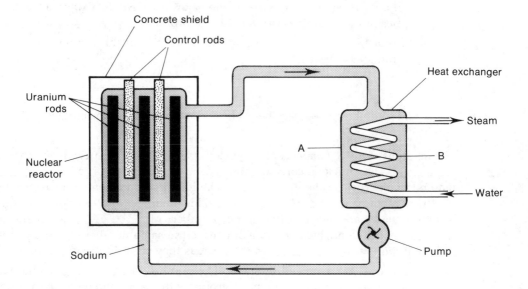

a)   Suggest why sodium is used and not potassium.

b)   What temperature must the reactor **not** reach? Explain your answer fully.

c)   What controls the temperature in the reactor?

d)   Using balanced equations to illustrate your answers, explain why it is extremely dangerous if a fault occurs in the piping

   i)   at A

   ii)   at B.

e)   i)   Draw the electronic structures of lithium, sodium and potassium.

   ii)   Use their electronic structures to explain the trend in their reaction with water.

f)   Caesium (Cs) is in the same group of the Periodic Table as sodium. Write a balanced equation, with state symbols, for the reaction of caesium with water.

g)   What colour would you expect caesium chloride to be? Give a reason for your answer.

h)   Rubidium is similar to potassium. Write a balanced equation, with state symbols, for the reaction of rubidium (Rb) with water.

i)   Draw the electronic structures of a sodium atom and a sodium ion.

j)   Explain, in terms of the electronic structures you drew in part i), why group 1 elements react violently with chlorine.

k)   Explain, in terms of their electronic structures, why there is an increase in the reactivity of the elements on descending group 1.

l)   Caesium (Cs) is an element in the first group of the Periodic Table.

   i)   Show, using outer electrons only, how you would expect an atom of caesium to combine with an atom of bromine.

   ii)   Predict, with reasons, *two* physical properties of the compound caesium bromide.

4   Copy and complete the passage below by adding the name of the particle(s) in each space.

Atoms consist of a small, central nucleus surrounded by negatively charged _____. The nucleus contains positively charged particles called _____ and neutral particles called _____. The identity of an element is determined by the number of _____ in its nucleus. In a neutral atom (one with no overall charge) there are always the same number of _____ as there are _____ in the nucleus. If two atoms have the same number of protons but a different number of _____ in the nucleus they are said to be isotopes.

The _____ are arranged in shells. The number of _____ in the outer shell of all elements in one of the main groups is the same, and equal to the group number. This is why elements in the same group have similar properties. To make an ion, one or more _____ must be gained or lost.

Theme 2

Chemical Changes

1 REACTIONS AND REACTIVITY

Types of Chemicals and Chemical Change

1 a) What is the difference between a **physical change** and a **chemical change**?

   b) Draw up a table with two headings, *Physical changes* and *Chemical changes*. Place each of the following in your table under the correct heading.

   water boiling   a bicycle going rusty
   petrol burning   food being digested
   sugar dissolving in water   methane mixing with air
   ice forming on a pond   chlorine bleaching litmus paper
   electricity flowing through copper wire   a resistor getting warm

2 a) Copy and complete the **fire triangle** by adding the missing ingredient:

   b) Which gas present in air is needed for combustion?

   c) Explain each of the following:

   i) A wet towel can be used to put out a fire in a chip pan.

   ii) Flammable liquids are often stored in an atmosphere of nitrogen.

   iii) Water should not be used to put out electrical fires.

   d) Explain why blowing hard on the base of a camp fire makes the wood burn more vigorously, but blowing hard on a match puts the flame out.

3 The experiment below demonstrates the combustion of petrol in a car engine.

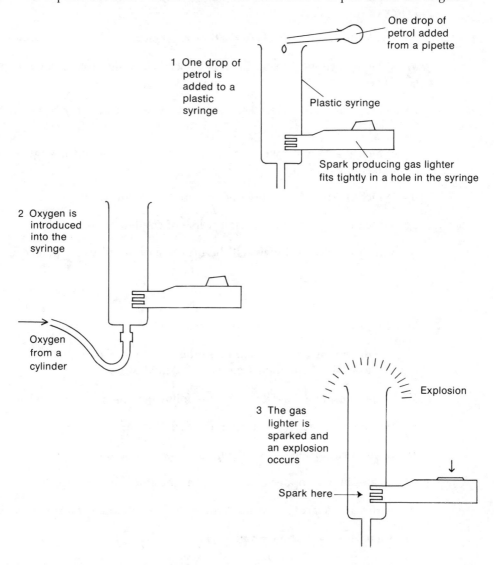

1 One drop of petrol is added to a plastic syringe

One drop of petrol added from a pipette

Plastic syringe

Spark producing gas lighter fits tightly in a hole in the syringe

2 Oxygen is introduced into the syringe

Oxygen from a cylinder

3 The gas lighter is sparked and an explosion occurs

Explosion

Spark here

a) From what naturally occurring material is petrol obtained?

b) Why should the syringes used in this experiment be made from plastic and not glass?

c) Which part of the car engine is represented by the gas lighter?

d) Acidic nitrogen oxides produced in car engines are pollutants. How are they formed?

e) Name the carbon compound produced when petrol burns in

   i)   a rich supply of oxygen

   ii) a poor supply of oxygen

4   In answering the following questions, choose one or more of the reaction types listed below:

       hydrolysis   **polymerisation**   **cracking**   **condensation**

a)   Which reaction(s) result in large molecules being broken down into smaller ones?

b)   Which reaction(s) result in small molecules being converted into larger ones?

c)   Which reaction(s) take place when starch is converted into glucose during digestion?

d)   Which reaction types describe the production of nylon?

e)   Which type of reaction is the reverse of condensation?

f)   Which reaction(s) involve(s) the breaking of bonds using water?

5   Some types of chemical reaction are listed below.

       decomposition   **neutralisation**   **combustion**
       oxidation/reduction (redox)   **dehydration**

Which reaction type best describes the following changes?

a)   hexane + oxygen $\longrightarrow$ carbon dioxide + water

b)   calcium carbonate $\longrightarrow$ calcium oxide + carbon dioxide

c)   magnesium + copper oxide $\longrightarrow$ magnesium oxide + copper

d)   hydrochloric acid + sodium hydroxide $\longrightarrow$ sodium chloride + water

e)   sucrose $\longrightarrow$ carbon + water

6 a) Ammonia is very soluble in water. Explain why method 1 (below) is unsuitable for producing ammonia solution, while method 2 works well.

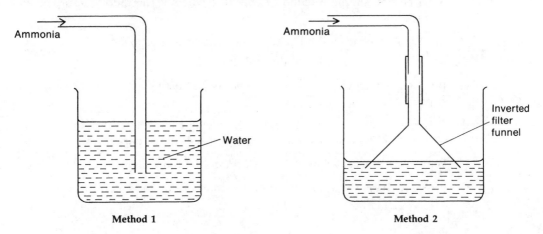

Method 1   Method 2

b) What effect does ammonia have on moist red litmus paper?

c) Why is concentrated sulphuric acid not used for drying ammonia? What is used instead?

d) Describe what happens when a piece of cotton wool soaked in ammonia is placed next to another soaked in hydrochloric acid, and name the compound formed.

7 The apparatus below is used to synthesise ammonia in the laboratory.

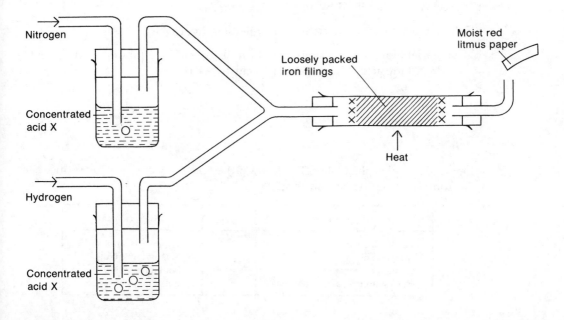

a) The gases are taken from cylinders, and must be supplied to the reaction vessel in the ratio 1 part nitrogen to 3 parts hydrogen. Using the apparatus as shown, describe one simple method of checking whether the ratio is approximately correct.

b) i)   What is 'concentrated acid X' and what is its purpose?

    ii)   What is the purpose of the iron filings?

c) If the experiment was successful, what would happen to the moist red litmus paper?

d) Describe another test for ammonia, involving concentrated hydrochloric acid, which could be used instead of the moist red litmus paper.

e) Why must this experiment be performed in a fume cupboard?

f) Name two *compounds* which produce ammonia when heated together.

8 The following statements refer to acids. Some are correct, others are incorrect. Copy them out, correcting those that are wrong.

a) Acidic solutions have a pH less than 7.

b) All substances which contain hydrogen are acids.

c) Weak acids that are safe to taste, taste sour.

d) Acidic solutions turn red litmus paper blue.

e) All acids contain the element hydrogen.

f) Acids are neutralised by alkalis.

g) Metal carbonates react with acids, releasing hydrogen.

h) Some laboratory acids and their formulae include sulphuric acid (H_2SO_4), hydrochloric acid (HCl) and nitric acid (NaOH).

9 Copy and complete the table below to show the acid you would use to produce each salt from the given starting material.

Starting material	Acid	Salt produced
Copper (II) oxide Magnesium Sodium carbonate Potassium hydroxide solution		Copper (II) sulphate Magnesium nitrate Sodium chloride Potassium phosphate

10 Magnesium sulphate can be prepared using the following steps, but *not* in the order shown.

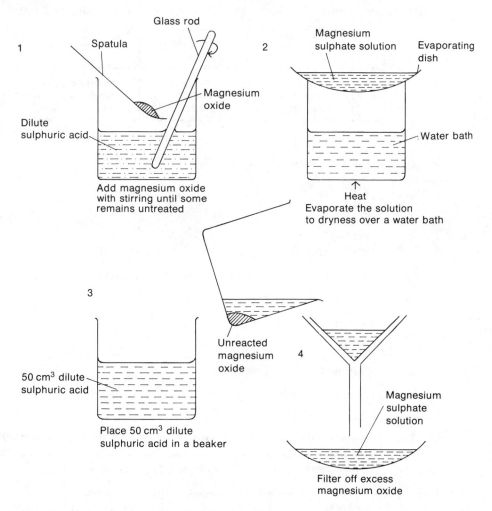

a) Draw the diagrams in the correct sequence.

b) Why is the magnesium oxide added until some remains unreacted?

c) Why is the solution heated to dryness using a water bath?

d) Using this method, powdered magnesium sulphate is obtained. How would you modify the method to obtain large crystals of magnesium sulphate?

e) An alternative method for producing magnesium sulphate involves adding magnesium ribbon to dilute sulphuric acid. Explain why this method, using the reaction between a metal and an acid, would *not* be suitable for making

   i)   copper (II) sulphate

   ii) sodium sulphate

f) What is the pH of magnesium sulphate solution?

11 The effect of three salts on water is shown in the table. Give brief details of the method you would use to prepare a sample of each salt from the starting material indicated. Explain why each method is suitable for that particular salt.

Salt	Effect of adding the salt to water	Starting material
Potassium sulphate	Dissolves	Potassium carbonate
Barium sulphate	Insoluble	Barium chloride solution
Aluminium chloride	Reacts	Aluminium

12 Look at the following pH ranges:

pH 1–3
pH 4–6
pH 7
pH 8–10
pH 11–13

Which pH range would apply to each of the following solutions?

a) concentrated sodium hydroxide solution

b) an antacid medicine

c) water

d) concentrated hydrochloric acid

e) dilute ammonia solution

13 The table below shows the pH at which some indicators undergo a colour change.

Indicator name	pH of solution at colour change	'Acid' colour	'Alkali' colour
Thymol blue	2	Red	Yellow
Bromophenol blue	4	Yellow	Blue
Methyl red	5	Red	Yellow
Phenol red	8	Yellow	Red
Phenolphthalein	9	Colourless	Red
Thymolphthalein	10	Colourless	Blue

a) Which indicator(s) would be red in a solution of pH 6?

b) Which indicator(s) could be used to distinguish between two samples, one of dilute ammonia solution (pH 9), the other of dilute sodium hydroxide solution (pH 12)?

c) What colour would bromophenol blue be in

i) a solution of pH 14?

ii) a solution of pH 4?

14 Copy and complete the following passage about acids and bases by filling in the missing word or words.

Acidic solutions have pH values between _____ and _____, while water-soluble bases (known as _____) have a pH between ____ and ____. Neutral solutions have a pH of _____. All acids contain the element _____, but it is NOT true that all compounds which contain this element are acids.

Common reactions of acids include the production of the gas _____ and a salt when added to reactive metals, formation of a salt, water and _____ when reacted with metal carbonates. The reaction between an acid and a base is known as _____, one example of this being the production of _____ _____ and _____ when hydrochloric acid reacts with sodium hydroxide solution. Bases produce the _____ ion when dissolved in water. This reacts with the _____ ion from acids during a neutralisation reaction.

Acid/base indicators are usually coloured compounds which can gain or lose _____ ions. When they do so, they undergo a colour change. An example of such an indicator is _____, which is _____ in acidic solutions and _____ in basic solutions.

15 Explain the following observations as fully as you can. Write word equations or balanced chemical equations for any reactions you mention, and use diagrams where necessary to illustrate your answer.

a) When 50 cm^3 0.1 M sodium hydroxide is mixed with 50 cm^3 of a 0.1 M solution of any of the common laboratory acids (sulphuric, hydrochloric or nitric acid) the temperature rise is the same.

b) A solution of hydrogen chloride dissolved in an organic solvent (e.g. methylbenzene) does not conduct electricity but an aqueous solution of the same gas does conduct electricity.

c) When dilute sulphuric acid is electrolysed, the volume of hydrogen produced is twice that of oxygen.

d) If a solution of hydrochloric acid (pH $=$ 3) was diluted with 10 000 times its own volume of water, what pH would it have?

16 When an alkali is added to an acid, the pH changes. The graph below shows the pH changes during the addition of 75 cm^3 of 0.1 M sodium hydroxide solution (alkali) to a sample of hydrochloric acid.

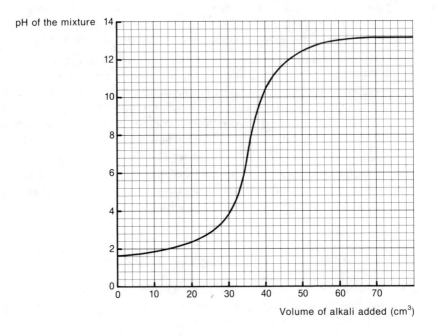

a)   What is the pH of the solution

    i)   at the start of the experiment?

    ii)   at the end of the experiment?

b)   What volume of alkali was added when the pH reached 7?

c)   The equation for the reaction between sodium hydroxide solution and hydrochloric acid is

    $NaOH(aq) + HCl(aq) \longrightarrow NaCl(aq) + H_2O(l)$

    i)   How many moles of HCl react exactly with 1 mole of NaOH?

    ii)   Explain how this experimental technique can be used to find the concentration of the hydrochloric acid.

17

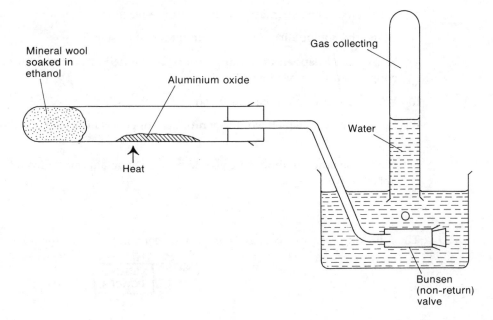

When heated and passed over hot aluminium oxide, ethanol is converted into ethene.

$$C_2H_5OH(g) \xrightarrow[Al_2O_3]{heat} C_2H_4(g) + H_2O(g)$$

a)   What is the role of aluminium oxide in this experiment?

b)   What *type* of reaction is this, in which water is removed from a compound?

c)   Explain how a Bunsen (non-return) valve works and why it is necessary.

d)   Ethene is an **unsaturated hydrocarbon**. What does this mean?

e)   Give details of a simple chemical test which can be used to distinguish between saturated and unsaturated hydrocarbons.

18   The ore **malachite** contains copper carbonate. The sequence of steps below were carried out by a student to demonstrate how copper can be obtained from malachite.

1. Heat powdered malachite in a hard glass test tube.
2. After cooling, stir the contents of the tube into warm, dilute sulphuric acid until some solid remains unreacted.
3. Filter the resulting solution.
4. Add an iron nail to the filtrate, then pour off the solution after a few minutes.

a)   Write down what you would *see* happening in step 1.

b)   Write a word equation for the reaction occurring in step 1.

c)   Explain why the solid was added until present *in excess* during step 2.

d)   What type of reaction occurred in step 2?

e)   Write a balanced chemical equation for the reaction in step 2.

f)   Name the compound present in the filtrate after step 3.

g)   What would happen to the appearance of the nail after step 4 showing that copper had been produced?

h)   What type of reaction has occurred in step 4?

i)   Name one metal which would *not* produce copper when added to the filtrate in step 4.

j)   Name one other method which could be used to obtain copper from the filtrate obtained from step 3.

19   The following reactions concern compounds containing the element copper.

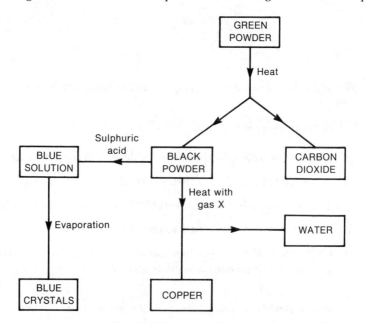

a)   Give the names of the following compounds.

   i)   Green powder: _____

   ii)   Black powder: _____

   iii) Blue crystals: _____

   iv)   Gas X: _____

b)   Write down the word equation for *one* reaction in this diagram which is a neutralisation.

c)   Write down a balanced chemical equation for *one* reaction in this diagram which is a reduction.

d)   Describe *one* way of obtaining copper from the blue crystals.

20

a) Using the information on the packet, calculate the number of grams in one ounce.

b) The crisps in this packet are surrounded by nitrogen, which is at just over one atmosphere pressure. Any air inside the packet would reduce the shelf-life of the crisps because of a reaction with the fat in the crisps.

> fat in crisps + air ⟶ aldehydes and organic acids
> (nasty smells and unpleasant taste)

   i)   Which gas present in air causes this reaction?
   ii) What type of reaction is this?

c) i)   Name one gas (other than nitrogen) present in air which would not react with the fat in crisps. Why is nitrogen chosen for use in preference to the gas you have named?

   ii) Give two advantages of having the nitrogen in the packet at a higher pressure than the atmosphere.

d) Why are flammable liquids usually transported in an atmosphere of nitrogen?

21   The following experiment was set up to find the conditions needed for iron to rust.

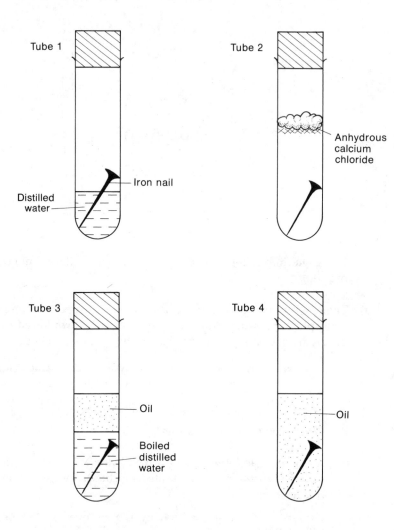

After setting up the tube as shown, they were left for two weeks.

a)   What was the purpose of the anhydrous calcium chloride in tube 2?

b)   Why was the water in tube 3

i)   distilled

ii)   boiled?

c)   What was the purpose of the oil layer in tube 3?

d)   The nail in tube 1 showed signs of rusting after two weeks, while the others did not. What conditions are needed for iron to rust?

e)   What was the purpose of tube 4?

f)   Explain how the rusting of iron can be classified as oxidation.

22 a) What is the chemical name for rust?

b) i) How does a layer of tin prevent rust forming on the inside of a can of fruit?

 ii) What would happen to the iron in the can if the can was damaged and some of the tin was removed from the inside?

c) Zinc blocks are attached to the steel hulls of ships, as shown in the diagram below.

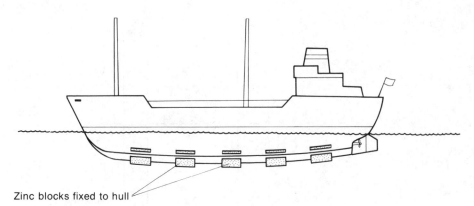

Zinc blocks fixed to hull

 i) How does the zinc protect the ship from rusting?

 ii) What would happen if copper blocks were used instead of zinc?

d) Name a metal which, when added to steel, produces a rust resistant alloy.

e) Describe one other method of preventing rusting. Explain how this method works.

23 a) Copy and complete the following table, which lists common definitions of oxidation and reduction.

Oxidation	Reduction
	Loss of oxygen
Loss of hydrogen	
	Gain of electrons

b) Use the table to decide whether the element in **bold type** in each of the following reactions has been oxidised or reduced.

 i) The extraction of iron in a blast furnace

$$\mathbf{Fe_2O_3} + 3CO \longrightarrow 2Fe + 3CO_2$$

 ii) The combustion of carbon monoxide above a coal fire

$$2CO + O_2 \longrightarrow 2CO_2$$

 iii) The production of aluminium at the cathode during electrolysis

$$\mathbf{Al^{3+}} + 3e^- \longrightarrow Al \quad (e^- = \text{an electron})$$

    iv) The reaction of sodium with water

$$2Na + 2H_2O \longrightarrow 2NaOH + H_2$$

    v) The reaction of lead with silver nitrate solution

$$Pb + 2AgNO_3 \longrightarrow Ag + Pb(NO_3)_2$$

c) Explain what is meant by a 'redox' reaction using one of the above reactions to illustrate your answer.

24

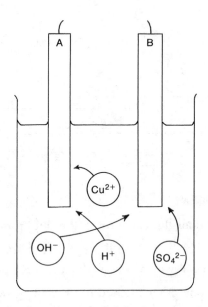

The above diagram shows the movement of the ions present during the electrolysis of copper sulphate solution. The electrodes A and B are connected to a d.c. power supply.

a) Which electrode is the anode? Explain your choice.

b) Which two of the ions shown combine to make water?

c) Which ions are attracted to the cathode during electrolysis?

d) Copy and complete the following table which lists the observations you would expect:

	Observations	
	Before start	*During electrolysis*
Anode	No change	
Cathode	No change	
Solution	Clear blue	Clear, paler blue

e) Why does the colour of the solution fade during electrolysis?

f) What would happen to the colour of the solution during electrolysis if both electrodes were made of copper? Explain your answer.

25 When a solution of copper(II) sulphate is electrolysed using graphite (carbon) electrodes, the following results are obtained.

Observations of		
anode	*cathode*	*the solution*
Gas evolved	Cathode coated with pink deposit	Blue colour fades, solution becomes acidic and warm

a) Name the gas evolved at the anode and the pink deposit at the cathode.

b) i) Which elements were present in the solution at the start?

ii) Which elements are removed during electrolysis?

iii) Explain why the blue colour fades

iv) Why does the solution become acidic?

c) Why does the temperature of the solution rise?

d) How would the results of the experiment differ if the electrodes were made of copper?

26 Lead iodide was placed in a crucible. The circuit shown below was set up and the power switched on. The bulb did not light up. Heating was begun and after a few minutes the lead iodide began to melt. Immediately the bulb lit up. Purple fumes could be seen coming from the anode, while silver coloured droplets appeared around the cathode. Heating was stopped and the contents of the crucible solidified. The bulb continued to glow.

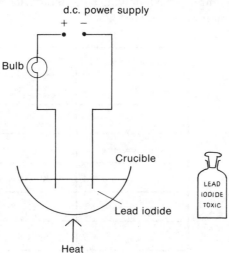

a) What *type* of particles are present in lead iodide?

b) Explain why the bulb lit up only when the lead iodide was molten.

c) Identify the purple fumes and the silvery-coloured droplets.

d) Explain why the bulb remained on after the contents of the crucible solidified.

e) What safety precautions are necessary during this experiment?

27 This question concerns the electrolysis of molten magnesium bromide.

Copy and complete the passage below, choosing the correct words from this list to fill in the blanks.

> bromine   magnesium   anode   cathode   decomposed
> lattice   ions   vibrate   move   electric current

The particles present in solid magnesium bromide are charged atoms called _____. As a solid, these particles can only _____ as they are fixed in a giant _____. Once the magnesium bromide is molten, the particles are free to _____ and can carry the _____. The positively charged particles of _____ are attracted to the _____, while the negatively charged particles of _____ are attracted to the _____. During electrolysis the compound is _____.

Chemical Tests

1 a) Describe how you would carry out a flame test on a sample of pure, solid potassium chloride to demonstrate the test result expected.

b) Copy and complete the following table, which describes the flame test result for some common metal ions:

Colour of flame	Ion probably present
Brick Red	
	Na^+
Apple green	
	K^+
Blue green	
	Sr^{2+}

2 A chemistry teacher notices that the labels have fallen off three bottles, known to contain magnesium sulphate, magnesium chloride and magnesium carbonate.

Explain in detail how she could carry out simple chemical test(s) to identify the contents of each bottle. For each test, give the name of the test solution(s) used, the result(s) you would expect, and a word equation for the reaction(s) involved.

3 Explain how you would use simple chemical tests to distinguish between samples of the following pairs of compounds.

For each test, describe the test reagent(s) needed, what you would do, and what result you would expect.

a) cyclohexene and cyclohexane

b) ethanol and ethanoic acid

c) ethanol and water

4

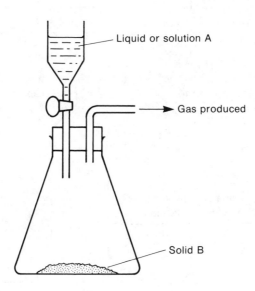

The apparatus shown above can be used to generate the gases oxygen, chlorine, hydrogen, hydrogen chloride and carbon dioxide, given suitable choices of A and B.

Copy the diagram, and the table below, and complete the table by giving the names of A and B.

Gas produced	A	B
Oxygen		
Hydrogen		
Chlorine		
Hydrogen chloride		
Carbon dioxide		

5   The diagram shows a key which can be used to identify some metal ions.

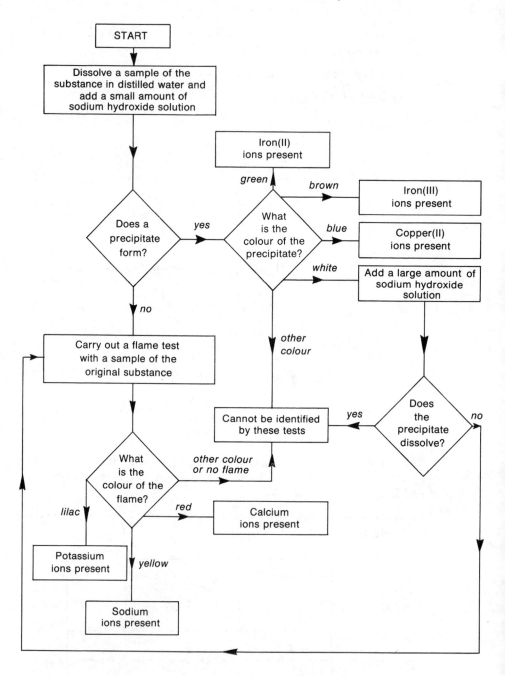

a)   What property must all the metal ions have if they are to be identified using this key?

b)   What is the name of the laboratory equipment that you could use to add only a few drops of sodium hydroxide solution to your dissolved sample?

c) Why should *distilled* water be used when dissolving the sample?

d) Use the key to identify as closely as possible the metal ion(s) present in each of the following compounds.

    i) No precipitate formed when a few drops of sodium hydroxide solution was added to an aqueous solution of the compound. A flame test was carried out on the original substance and the flame turned to a lilac colour.

    ii) A white precipitate formed when a few drops of sodium hydroxide solution was added to an aqueous solution of the compound. This precipitate then dissolved when more sodium hydroxide solution was added.

e) The addition of sodium hydroxide solution to an aqueous solution of iron (III) chloride results in the chemical reaction described below:

iron (III)   + sodium   sodium   + iron (III)
chloride (aq)   hydroxide (aq) $\longrightarrow$ chloride (x)   hydroxide (y)

where x and y refer to the state.

If all sodium compounds are soluble in water, then using only this and the information in the key, answer the following questions.

    i) What is the state symbol which should be used for x?

    ii) What is the state symbol which should be used for y?

6 Copy and complete the following table, which shows chemical tests for some gases.

Name of the gas	Description of the test	What you would expect in a positive result
Oxygen		
Hydrogen		
Chlorine		
Carbon dioxide		
Ammonia		
Hydrogen chloride		

The Reactivity Series

1 The following is part of the reactivity series for metals. (Hydrogen is included, although it is a gaseous non-metal.)

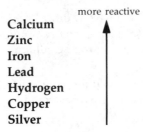

more reactive

Calcium
Zinc
Iron
Lead
Hydrogen
Copper
Silver

a) Use the list to predict the outcome of the following reactions. For those instances when you think reaction will occur, write a word equation to show what happens.

   i) Iron(III) oxide is heated with lead granules.

   ii) Lead foil is added to silver nitrate solution.

   iii) Zinc powder is heated with calcium oxide.

   iv) Copper is added to dilute hydrochloric acid.

   v) Zinc is added to dilute hydrochloric acid.

b) Explain why the elements at the bottom of the series were discovered before the elements at the top.

2 The metals in the list below are in order of increasing reactivity:

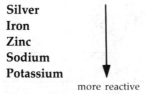

Silver
Iron
Zinc
Sodium
Potassium

more reactive

a) Which metal in the list is found native (uncombined)?

b) Why is sodium not found native?

c) Zinc can be obtained from zinc oxide by heating it with carbon. Name one other metal from the list which is extracted in this way.

d) What type of process is used to extract reactive metals such as sodium?

e) Write separate word equations for the reaction of sodium with oxygen, water and chlorine.

f) What would happen if a zinc rod was placed in silver nitrate solution?

g) Magnesium will react with zinc oxide but not potassium oxide. Sodium is more reactive than magnesium. Rewrite the list with magnesium in the correct place.

3 Displacement reactions take place when a more reactive metal is put into a solution containing a salt of a less reactive metal. The table below shows the effect of adding three metals separately to solutions of other metal salts.

Metal added	Metal salt solution		
	X salt	Y salt	Z salt
X	No change	No change	No change
Y	Metal X displaced	No change	Metal Z displaced
Z	Metal X displaced	No change	No change

a) Write the letters of the three metals in order of reactivity, putting the *most* reactive *first*.

b) Give *two* changes you would *see* when excess magnesium is added to copper sulphate solution.

4 For each of the following situations, say whether you would expect any chemical reaction to occur. Assume that all solutions are in water.

For any predicted reactions, describe what you would expect to see and give a word equation for the reaction.

a) Chlorine is bubbled through a solution of sodium bromide.

b) Iodine solution is mixed with a solution of potassium bromide.

c) Copper oxide powder is heated with zinc powder.

d) Copper powder is added to dilute hydrochloric acid.

e) A piece of zinc foil is added to silver nitrate solution.

Rate of Reaction

1 Chemical reactions take place at a variety of rates. Some take less than a second, others a few minutes or hours, and some take place extremely slowly over many days.

Draw up a table with three headings, 'fast', 'moderate' and 'slow', and place each of the following reactions in your table under one of the headings. Justify your choice in each case.

> **Dynamite exploding**
> **Digestion of food in the body**
> **A dye fading in sunlight**
> **Toast burning**
> **The rusting of iron in a bicycle**
> **A silver trophy oxidising in air**
> **Petrol burning in a car engine**
> **Mortar hardening in air**
> **Baking a cake**
> **The formation of a precipitate, when solutions of silver nitrate and sodium chloride are mixed**

2 a) Copy and label the diagram below which shows the apparatus used to study the rate of reaction between marble chips (calcium carbonate) and dilute hydrochloric acid.

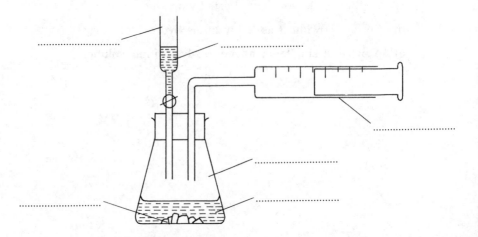

b) The following readings were taken during the experiment.

Time (s)	0	15	30	45	60	75	90	120	150	180	210	240	270
Volume of gas collected (cm^3)	0	7.0	15.1	27.2	38.9	54.0	70.1	94.2	108.1	115.4	118.6	120.0	120.0

       i) Name the gas produced in this reaction.

      ii) Plot a graph of volume of gas collected (cm^3) on the y-axis against time on the x-axis. Draw a smooth curve through the points.

c) At what time was the rate of reaction greatest? How did you decide?

d) When did the reaction stop?

e) On the same graph sketch the curve you would expect to obtain if the experiment was repeated using the same mass of *powdered* calcium carbonate.

f) Describe how you could follow the rate of this reaction without measuring the volume of gas produced. Draw a labelled diagram of your apparatus, and state what readings you would take.

3 a) 0.5 g magnesium ribbon is added to a 250 cm^3 beaker containing 100 cm^3 dilute hydrochloric acid. A reaction occurs, producing magnesium chloride solution and hydrogen gas. Which of the following changes would *increase* the rate of reaction?

       i) warming the acid prior to adding the magnesium
      ii) carrying out the reaction in a 150 cm^3 beaker
     iii) using the same mass of powdered magnesium
     iv) using 200 cm^3 acid of the same concentration
      v) using 100 cm^3 concentrated hydrochloric acid

b) Draw a labelled diagram of the apparatus you would use to measure the rate of reaction in this experiment.

4 When sodium thiosulphate solution reacts with dilute hydrochloric acid, a precipitate of sulphur forms.

$$Na_2S_2O_3(aq) + 2HCl(aq) \longrightarrow 2NaCl(aq) + H_2O(l) + SO_2(g) + S(s)$$

To study the effect of temperature on the rate of the reaction, Neil mixed 50 cm^3 sodium thiosulphate at 20 °C with 10 cm^3 dilute hydrochloric acid, in a conical flask. The flask was placed on a piece of paper, which had a cross drawn on it. Neil timed how long it took for the cross to disappear as seen by looking down through the flask.

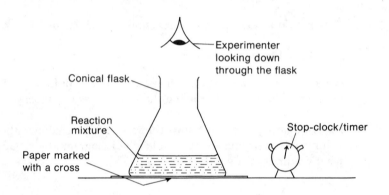

After writing down the time, he repeated the experiment with both solutions at a higher temperature. The results he obtained are given in the table below.

Temperature (°C)	Time taken for the cross to disappear (t) in seconds	1/t
20	198	0.005
30	97	0.010
40	48	0.021
50	28	0.036
60	20	0.050

a) i) Name all the products of the reaction.

ii) What caused the cross to disappear?

b) What effect does raising the temperature have on the rate of reaction?

c) Neil calculated values of 1/t, where t is the time taken for the cross to disappear. Explain how this value gives a direct measure of the rate of reaction.

d) A 'rule of thumb' regarding rates of reaction states that the rate of a 'well-behaved' reaction doubles for every 10 °C rise in temperature.

i) Do the results of this experiment agree with the rule of thumb?

ii) Is the reaction well-behaved throughout the temperature range used?

5 Enzymes are an important group of proteins. Choose words from this list to complete the following sentences about enzymes.

> catalysts   destroyed   neutral   organisms   proteins
> reactions   specific

a) Enzymes are _____ which speed up the chemical _____ which occur in _____. They are 'biological _____'.

b) Enzymes are _____ in that they can only control one type of reaction.

c) Enzymes are _____ by excess heat and are also sensitive to changes in pH. Most enzymes work best in _____ conditions.

6 Copy and complete the table, which compares enzymes with non-biological catalysts.

Enzymes	Non-biological catalysts
Usually catalyse only one reaction	
	Work well at a range of temperatures
	Only small quantities are needed

7 Hydrogen peroxide can be broken down by catalysts into water and oxygen. In an experiment to investigate this reaction, samples of fresh and previously boiled materials were added to samples of hydrogen peroxide in test tubes. Any gas evolved was tested for oxygen. The results are shown below.

Test tube	Contents	Test on gas evolved
1	Hydrogen peroxide	No oxygen evolved
2	Hydrogen peroxide + fresh manganese dioxide	Oxygen evolved
3	Hydrogen peroxide + boiled manganese dioxide	Oxygen evolved
4	Hydrogen peroxide + fresh liver	Oxygen evolved
5	Hydrogen peroxide + boiled liver	No oxygen evolved
6	Hydrogen peroxide + fresh blood	Oxygen evolved
7	Hydrogen peroxide + boiled blood	No oxygen evolved

a) What would you see happening in the test tubes as gas is evolved?

b) How would you test the gas for oxygen?

c) Why was Tube 1 set up?

d) Explain carefully what has happened in Tube 2.

e) Explain the results which occur in tubes 4 and 6.

f) Explain why the result obtained in Tube 3 differs from that in Tubes 5 and 7.

g) State *two* factors which should be kept constant in all seven tubes.

8 When magnesium ribbon reacts with excess dilute sulphuric acid, a salt and a gas are formed. The following investigation is used to find out how the pH of the acid solution affects the speed of the reaction. Magnesium ribbon is added to sulphuric acid of different concentrations and to water alone, as shown below.

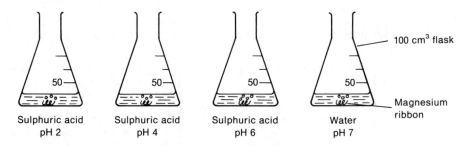

| Sulphuric acid | Sulphuric acid | Sulphuric acid | Water |
| pH 2 | pH 4 | pH 6 | pH 7 |

100 cm³ flask

Magnesium ribbon

a) What volume of liquid is used in each beaker?

b) What piece of apparatus would you use to measure out the liquid accurately?

c) In which acid solution would the magnesium react fastest? Explain why this acid solution reacts fastest with the magnesium. Use a particle model of chemical reactions in your answer.

9 Each of the following graphs has 'time' plotted on the *x*-axis.

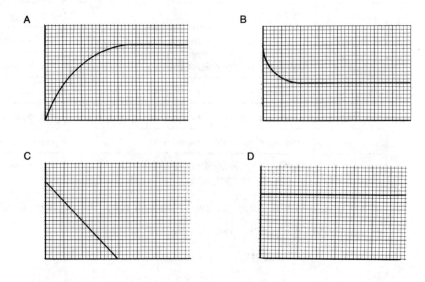

A

B

C

D

E

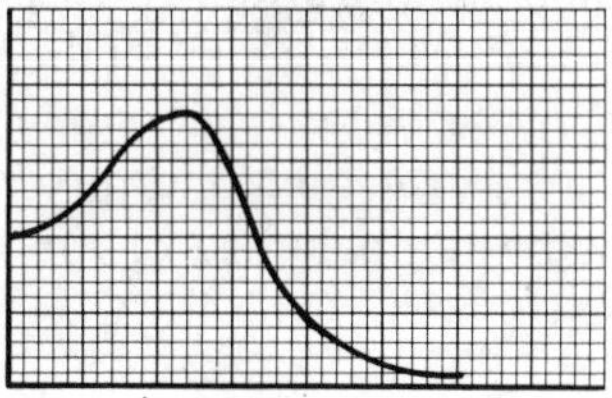

Which graph would you expect to obtain when the following are plotted along the y-axis?

a) The volume of carbon dioxide produced when marble chips (calcium carbonate) react with excess hydrochloric acid solution.

b) The mass of a flask containing zinc granules reacting with excess hydrochloric acid solution.

c) The mass of manganese dioxide catalyst during the catalytic decomposition of a solution of hydrogen peroxide.

d) The rate of reaction in a process where one of the products is a catalyst for the reaction.

Energy Transfer

1 a) Here are some energy sources:

     coal   **water waves**   **oil**   **Sun**   **natural gas**   **wind**

List those energy sources which may be in short supply in the next few hundred years.

b) In Britain most of our electricity is generated in power stations using fossil fuels.

    i) Name two fossil fuels from the list in part a).

    ii) Give *two* ways burning fossil fuels in power stations causes problems in the environment.

2   A type of disposable hand warmer consists of a polythene container surrounding a powdered compound. At the centre of the hand warmer is a second polythene bag, much thinner than the outer layer, containing water. When the hand warmer is squeezed, the water is released and mixed with the powder. A chemical reaction takes place, and the temperature of the hand warmer rises. During a trial, the temperature rose from 21 °C to 48 °C in 5 minutes.

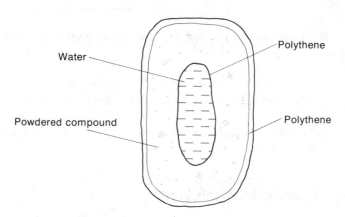

a) What was the rise in temperature of the hand warmer during the trial?

b) Is the reaction between the powdered compound and water exothermic or endothermic?

c) The table below shows the energy change in joules per gram, for four compounds A–D on reaction with water.

Compound	Energy change (J/g) on reaction with water
A	+312
B	−468
C	+68
D	−892

   i)   Which of the compounds would be suitable for use in the hand warmer?

   ii) Suggest one factor, other than the energy change on reaction with water, which would influence the choice of compound.

d) One compound which could be used in the hand warmer is calcium oxide, CaO. It reacts with water according to the following equation.

$$CaO\,(s) + H_2O\,(l) \longrightarrow Ca(OH)_2\,(s) + heat$$

This reaction can be reversed by heating the product.

   i)   Name the product of the reaction.

   ii) What hazards, if any, are there in using a hand warmer containing calcium oxide?

3

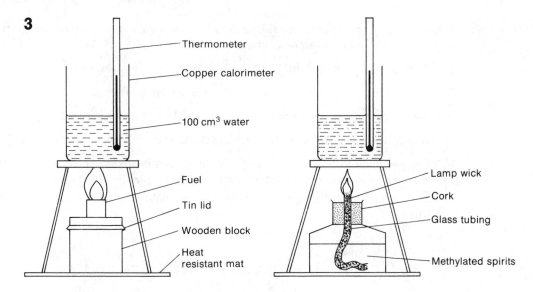

Alan carried out the following experiment to compare methylated spirits with solid fuel pellets for use with a small camping cooker. The solid fuel was burnt on a tin lid, while the methylated spirits was used in a wick burner. The mass of each fuel needed to raise the temperature of 100 cm^3 water through $20 \degree C$ was found.

Results obtained in the experiment are given below.

        Initial water temperature $19 \degree C$
        Final water temperature $39 \degree C$
        Mass of lid plus fuel (start) 25.30 g
        Mass of lid plus fuel (end) 23.50 g
        Cost of solid fuel (500 g) £4.00

        Initial water temperature $19 \degree C$
        Final water temperature $39 \degree C$
        Mass of burner plus spirit (start) 120.25 g
        Mass of burner plus spirit (end) 119.45 g
        Cost of methylated spirits (200 g) 50p

a)   Why is a copper calorimeter used, rather than a glass beaker?

b)   Calculate the cost in pence per gram of each fuel.

c)   What mass of

     i)   solid fuel and

     ii) methylated spirits

   is needed to produce a $20 \degree C$ rise in the temperature of 100 cm^3 water?

d)   Which fuel is the best buy? Show how you arrived at your answer.

e)   Write down two advantages and one disadvantage (apart from cost) of each fuel for use with a portable cooker.

4 A good rocket propellant, consisting of a fuel and an oxidiser, must satisfy the following requirements, among others:

1. The reaction between fuel and oxidiser must be very fast.

2. The reaction between fuel and oxidiser must be exothermic.

One useful propellant uses hydrogen peroxide (H_2O_2) and hydrazine (N_2H_4).

a) Which of these two substances acts as the oxidiser? Explain your choice.

b) The products of the reaction between hydrogen peroxide and hydrazine are nitrogen and water. Write a balanced chemical equation for the reaction.

c) The energy level diagram shows the starting materials for this reaction being atomised.

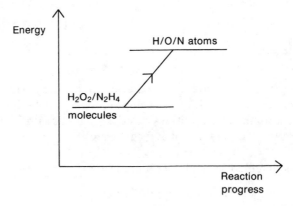

Copy and complete the diagram by showing the conversion of the atoms into the actual products of the reaction.

5 A student investigated three liquid fuels. Each fuel was used to heat 100 g samples of water.

The table shows the results of burning *three* 1 g samples of different liquid fuels.

Liquid fuel sample	Starting temperature of water (°C)	Final temperature of water (°C)
X	22	42
Y	24	42
Z	20	38

a) Which *one* of the three liquid fuel samples produced the most exothermic reaction?

b) Explain what is meant by

i) exothermic reaction

ii) endothermic reaction

6 Cyclohexene is a hydrocarbon and has the formula C_6H_{10}.

Cyclohexene reacts with hydrogen to form cyclohexane.

The following table gives bond energies for the chemical bonds found in cyclohexene, cyclohexane and hydrogen:

Bond	Bond energy (kJ/mol)
C—C	350
C=C	600
C—H	410
H—H	440

a) Calculate the total energy needed to break all the bonds in 1 mole of cyclohexene and 1 mole of hydrogen.

b) Calculate the total energy released by the formation of all the bonds when 1 mole of cyclohexane molecules is produced.

c) Use your answers to a) and b) to predict the overall energy change for this reaction. Say whether the reaction is exothermic or endothermic.

7 The following table gives approximate bond energies for three covalent bonds.

Bond	Bond energy (kJ/mol^{-1})
H—H	435
Cl—Cl	240
H—Cl	430

Calculate the energy change for the following processes, indicating clearly whether they are exothermic or endothermic:

a) $H_2(g) + Cl_2(g) \longrightarrow 2HCl(g)$

b) $HCl(g) \longrightarrow H(g) + Cl(g)$

8 The diagram below shows how the potential energy of the chemicals changes during the course of a chemical reaction. It shows the energy level of the reactants, the size of the activation energy and the energy level of the products.

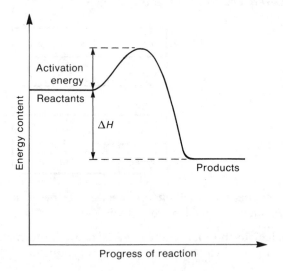

a) What is meant by 'activation energy'?

b) The potential energy of the products is lower than that of the reactants. What happens to this 'lost' energy?

c) What is the name given to this type of energy change?

d) Sketch on the diagram the change in potential energy for the same reaction taking place in the presence of a catalyst. Use this sketch to explain, in terms of energy levels, why catalysts are often used in industrial processes.

e) What name is given to the quantity labelled ΔH in the diagram?

Equilibrium

1 a) Explain what is meant by *chemical equilibrium*.

b) Ammonia is a poisonous gas which is easily turned into a liquid. It is produced by combining nitrogen gas and hydrogen gas. The rate of production depends on the pressure applied to the mixture and on the temperature at which the reaction is carried out, but not the equilibrium position.

The set of graphs in the diagram opposite shows these effects.

Use the set of graphs to help you answer the following questions.

i) What is the percentage yield of ammonia produced at a temperature of 450 °C and a pressure of 35 MPa?

ii) Describe the pattern linking the percentage yield of ammonia to the pressure.

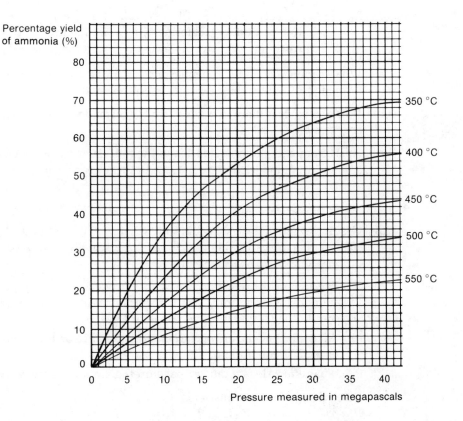

iii) Suggest what a manufacturer of ammonia should do to

the temperature and

the pressure

to increase the percentage yield of ammonia.

iv) The conditions usually used are a temperature of 400 °C and a pressure of 20 MPa. Without changing these conditions suggest *one* way in which the yield of ammonia might be increased.

2   If chlorine gas is passed over a sample of solid iodine, a brown liquid is formed. When the flow of chlorine is continued, orange crystals are formed on the side of the tube and the volume of brown liquid present decreases. If the flow of chlorine is stopped, the mass of orange solid decreases and the volume of brown liquid increases. These changes can be repeated by altering the amount of chlorine flowing over the brown liquid. Once formed, the brown liquid remains in the tube when excess chlorine has been removed.

The reactions taking place are as follows:

1. $$Cl_2 \quad + \quad I_2 \quad \longrightarrow \quad 2ICl$$
   chlorine +   iodine   iodine chloride
   (green gas)   (grey solid)   (brown liquid)

2. $$ICl \quad + \quad Cl_2 \quad \rightleftharpoons \quad ICl_3$$
   iodine chloride + chlorine   iodine trichloride
   (brown liquid)   (green gas)   (orange solid)

a)   What evidence is there, in the description of the experiment, to show that the formation of iodine chloride (ICl) is not reversible?

b)   What evidence is there to suggest that the formation of iodine trichloride (ICl_3) is reversible?

c)   Apart from adding more chlorine to the tube, suggest *one* way of changing the amount of iodine trichloride present in this experiment.

3   The following questions are about aspects of equilibrium.

a)   Gases are generally less soluble in warm water than cold water. Does this suggest that gases dissolving in water are usually *exothermic* or *endothermic* processes? Explain your answer.

b) i)   The reversible reaction between nitrogen and hydrogen to produce ammonia is exothermic. To increase the yield of ammonia at equilibrium, should the temperature be raised or lowered?

ii)   What effect would an increase in pressure have on the amount of ammonia formed at equilibrium?

iii) What effect does a catalyst have on the amount of ammonia formed?

Give reasons for your answers.

2 MAKING NEW MATERIALS

Structure, Bonding and Properties

1   a)   Copy and complete the following table, which shows examples of the four main types of material.

	Metals	Glasses/ ceramics	Plastics	Composites
Example	Iron		Nylon	
Large-scale use				
Properties important in this use				
Other useful properties				

b)   Which of the materials you have listed would be best for making the following items? Explain your choice.

i)   frying pan handle

ii)   dustbin

iii)   door handle

2   The diagrams below show the structure of graphite and diamond – alloptropes of carbon.

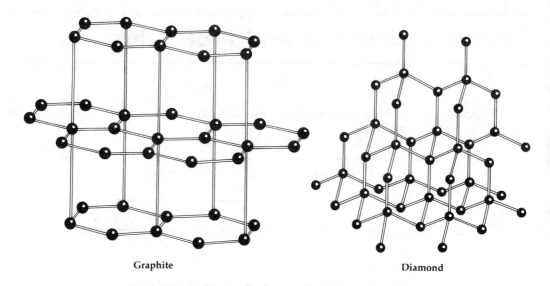

Graphite   Diamond

a)   What are allotropes?

b)   Copy and complete the following statements by choosing the correct word from the brackets. Use the diagrams above to help you.

i)   In a diamond, each of the carbon atoms forms four strong (covalent/ionic) bonds to other atoms in a (giant/layer) lattice. Although diamond is one of the hardest substances known, it is (malleable/brittle) because the forces between atoms act in a particular direction. As all four outer (electrons/ protons) in each (atom/molecule) are used in bonding, diamond is an electrical (insulator/conductor).

ii) Graphite has a structure in which each carbon atom forms (three/four) bonds to other atoms. The forces within each layer of atoms are (strong/ weak), while the forces between layers are (strong/weak). This is why the layers slide over each other easily, and explains the use of graphite as a (lubricant/adhesive). Because there is one (proton/electron) on each atom which is not used in bonding, graphite is an electrical (insulator/conductor).

3   The table below shows some information about four different substances. Use it to answer the questions which follow.

Substance	Does it conduct electricity		Does it have a high melting point?
	when solid?	when liquid?	
A	No	No	Yes
B	Yes	Yes	Yes
C	No	No	No
D	No	Yes	Yes

a)   Make a key to identify the four substances.

b)   Which of the substances A, B, C and D is most likely to be

   i)   a metal

   ii) a giant ionic structure

   iii) made from small molecules?

c) i)   Describe what is meant by a giant ionic structure.

   ii) Give one example of an everyday solid which has a giant ionic structure.

4   The following table lists some properties of the five substances V–Z.

Substance	Melting point	Solubility in water	Electrical conductivity		
			Solid	Liquid	Dissolved in water
V	Low	Very soluble	Nil	Nil	Good
W	Low	Insoluble	Nil	Nil	–
X	High	Insoluble	Good	Good	–
Y	High	Very soluble	Nil	Good	Good
Z	Low	Reacts	Good	Good	–

a)   Which of the substances are metals?

b)   Which of the substances has a giant ionic structure?

c)   Which of the substances is present as ions only when dissolved in water?

d)   Which substance could be sodium?

e)   Which substance could be hydrogen chloride?

5 The diagrams below show the structure of five solids, A–E.

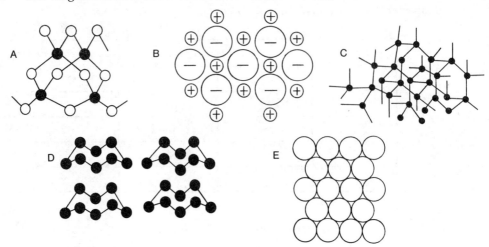

a) Which of the substances are elements?

b) Write down the letter of one substance which has

   i)   a giant structure

   ii) a molecular structure

c) Which substance will have the lowest melting point? Explain your choice.

d) Which letter could represent the structure of iron?

e) Write down the letter of one substance which

   i)   conducts electricity only when molten or dissolved in water

   ii) conducts electricity as a solid

6 The arrangement of long-chain molecules in low density (A) and high density (B) polyethene can be represented as shown in the diagrams below.

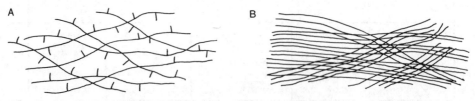

During the process which produces low density polyethene, side chains form which prevent the molecules from packing together more closely. The high density form is more rigid and does not soften at temperatures below 100 °C.

a) Using labelled copies of the diagrams, explain the difference in density between the two types of polythene.

b) Which form would you expect to have the greatest mechanical strength? Give your reasons.

c) Which type of polyethene would be more suitable for the following applications?

    i)   a washing up bowl

    ii) a carrier bag

    iii) a felt-tip pen

d) Explain why a carrier bag made from polyethene is a greater potential hazard to the environment than one made from paper.

7 The arrangement of molecules in a **thermosoftening** plastic differs from that in a **thermosetting** plastic. Molecular chains in the thermoset are cross-linked, a feature which affects the properties of the plastic.

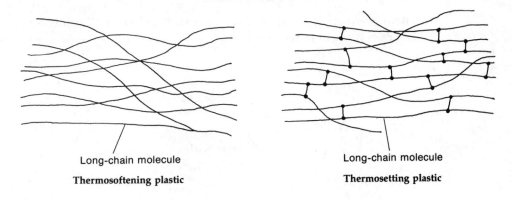

Long-chain molecule   Long-chain molecule

Thermosoftening plastic   **Thermosetting plastic**

a) Name one thermosoftening and one thermosetting plastic.

b) Copy and complete the following table, which compares the properties of thermosoftening and thermosetting plastics.

Thermosoftening	*Thermosetting*
	Hard and brittle
Soften and melt on heating	
Soluble in organic solvents	

8 Polyethene and polyphenylethene (polystyrene) are in widespread use as plastics. The structural formulae of the polymers are shown below.

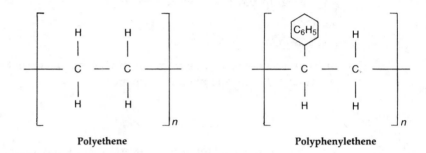

Polyethene   Polyphenylethene

a) What does n mean in these formulae?

b) Both polymers are made from alkenes such as ethene. Which bond in alkenes enables them to polymerise?

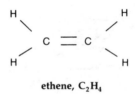

ethene, C_2H_4

c) Polyethene is more elastic than polyphenylethene (polystyrene). How does the different shape of the long-chain molecules in each polymer explain this difference?

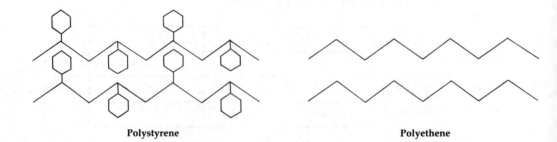

Polystyrene   Polyethene

d) i) Name the products formed when polyethene burns in a plentiful supply of air.

   ii) What problems are associated with disposing of waste polyethene by burning it?

9 The following items are now made from a polymer (plastic) rather than the traditional material listed. Copy the table and add two advantages and one disadvantage of the new material over the old.

Item	Old material	New material	Advantages	Disadvantage
Drainpipe	Ferrous metal	Polyvinyl chloride (PVC)	Does not corrode, easily cut	Not as tough
Chair	Wood	Polypropylene		
Wire insulation	Rubber	PVC		
Carrier bag	Paper	Polyethene		
Packaging	Straw	Polystyrene		
Rope	Jute	Nylon		

10 The three types of strong bonds found in solids are *covalent, ionic* and *metallic*.

Copy and complete the following table of substances which contain such bonds, and their properties.

	Covalent	Ionic	Metallic
Name of an element or compound which contains this bonding			
Does this element or compound conduct electricity as a solid?			
Does this element or compound conduct electricity when molten or dissolved in water?			
Is this element or compound soluble in water?			

11 a) What is meant by a *property* of an element or compound?

b) This list shows some properties shown by elements and compounds:

    A   solid at room temperature
    B   liquid at room temperature
    C   gas at room temperature
    D   conductor of electricity as a solid
    E   conductor of electricity only as a liquid or when dissolved in water
    F   non-conductor of electricity
    G   soluble in water
    H   insoluble in water
    I   reacts with water

For each of the following substances write down three letters (A–I) which show its properties. One example has been done for you.

sodium	A	D	I
sulphur	___	___	___
mercury	___	___	___
carbon dioxide	___	___	___
sodium chloride	___	___	___
ethanol	___	___	___
glucose	___	___	___
carbon (graphite)	___	___	___

12 Use ideas about *particles, structure* and *bonding* to explain the following observations. Draw diagrams where they would help to explain your answer.

a) When you hit a piece of sodium with a hammer, the metal changes shape but does not break, but when you hit a large crystal of sodium chloride with a hammer, the crystal shatters.

b) Sodium conducts electricity as a solid and when molten, while sodium chloride only conducts electricity when molten or dissolved in water.

c) Sodium reacts with water, while sodium chloride does not.

Chemicals in Our Lives

1 From the list of household chemicals, choose
  a) an antacid medicine
  b) a painkiller
  c) a bleach
  d) a solution of a dilute acid
  e) an alkaline gas in solution
  f) a sedative
  g) a gaseous fuel
  h) a carbohydrate
  i) a polymer
  j) a neutral salt

> **sodium hydrogen carbonate**   **aspirin**   **sodium chlorate (I)**
> **vinegar**   **ammonia**   **ethanol**   **methane**   **glucose**
> **polystyrene**   **sodium chloride**

2 The information on two common fertilisers is given in the table below:

Name	Formula	Solubility in water
Ammonium nitrate	NH_4NO_3	Dissolves readily
Urea	CON_2H_4	Dissolves slowly

  a) How many atoms are there in one formula unit of ammonium nitrate?
  b) Which element is responsible for the fertilising action of these compounds?
  c) Explain why there is an ever-increasing demand for fertilisers.
  d) Write down one method of fertilising soil which does not involve man-made chemicals.
  e) What property of urea makes it a slow acting fertiliser?
  f) Which acid must be reacted with ammonia to make ammonium nitrate?
  g) Give one problem which might arise from the direct use of ammonia solution as a fertiliser.
  h) The large-scale use of fertilisers has given rise to some environmental problems. Briefly describe two of these.

3 A mixture of ammonium nitrate and calcium carbonate, known as nitrochalk, is often used on acidic soil. Explain how this mixture fertilises soil and reduces the acidity.

4 Read the passage below, then answer the questions which follow.

> Some phosphorus-containing insecticides are in use today to rid crops of pests. Many are also toxic to mammals, so great care must be taken in choosing a safe insecticide. Some have such a high toxicity that only 0.000 01 g per kg body mass is fatal to humans.
>
> When applied to plants, these insecticides become part of the plant's system and are very effective in killing insects all over the plant. One such compound, called malathion, has proved to be useful in treating head lice infestation in humans. Malathion has a high toxicity to insects but low toxicity to mammals. Unfortunately, it smells of rotten cabbages! The structural formula of malathion is given below.

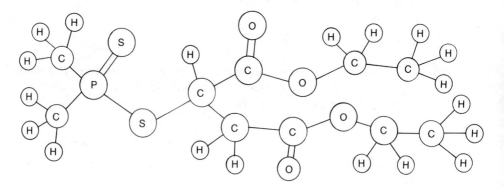

a) Why are phosphorus-based insecticides potentially dangerous?

b) Is the type of plant insecticide discussed in the passage best described as local or systemic? Explain your choice.

c) If an insecticide has a toxicity of 0.000 01 g/kg body mass, what is the minimum amount which would be fatal to a 70 kg man?

d) State one advantage and one disadvantage of the insecticide malathion for treating head lice infestation.

e) Substitute numerical values for v, w, x, y and z in the molecular formula for malathion:

$$C_v \; H_w \; P_x \; S_y \; O_z$$

5 a) Copy and complete the table below, which gives examples of some types of drug and their effect on the body.

Effect on the body	Type	Example
Analgesic		Kills pain
Antacid	Sodium hydrogencarbonate	
Anaesthetic		
	Penicillin	
	Caffeine	Keeps you awake and active
	Ethanol (alcohol)	
	LSD	Causes hallucinations

6 The molecules of two drugs, aspirin and caffeine, are shown below.

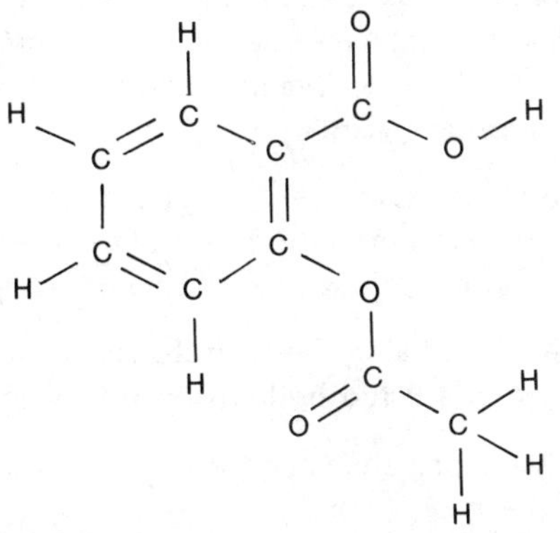

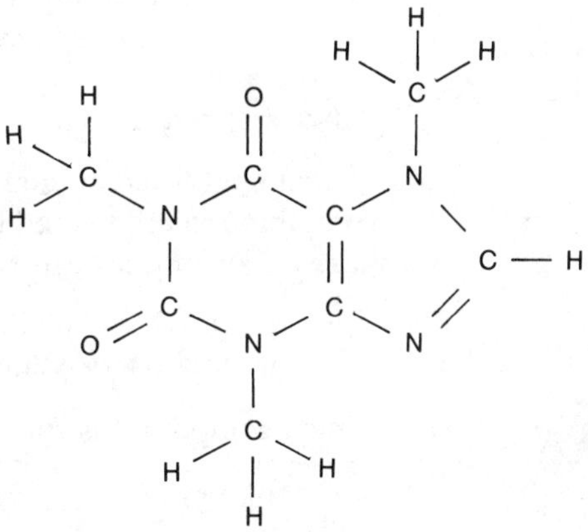

a) What is the difference between a drug and a medicine?

b) How many bonds do the atoms of

    i) hydrogen

    ii) oxygen

    iii) nitrogen

    iv) carbon

    form with other atoms in these molecules?

c) Write down the molecular formulae of aspirin and caffeine.

d) What action do *each* of these drugs have on the body?

e) Name two drinks which contain caffeine.

7 For almost 100 years, the only anaesthetics in use were nitrous oxide (N_2O), ether ($C_4H_{10}O$) and chloroform ($CHCl_3$). None of these is very effective, and each has a number of disadvantages. Nitrous oxide does not put patients into a deep sleep some operating theatres which used ether were destroyed in explosions or fires, and chloroform is believed to cause damage to the heart and liver.

Research during the last 50 years has produced a number of highly successful anaesthetics. Some compounds with anaesthetic properties are listed in the table below.

Molecular formula of the compound	Boiling point/°C	LD_{50}	Percentage halogen content by mass
$CHCl_3$	61	2.6	89
$CHFCl_2$	9	6.4	87
CF_3CHBr_2	73	2.0	90
$CF_3CHClBr$	50	3.6	87
$CHFClCF_2OCHF_2$	57	8.0	71

a) i) What is a halogen?

ii) Compounds containing carbon, hydrogen and halogens are more likely to cause explosions as the halogen content decreases. Place the compounds in the table in order of increasing risk of explosion during use, and indicate clearly which is the most dangerous.

b) The number listed under the heading LD_{50} is the percentage concentration of the compound in air needed to kill 50% of a sample of mice ('LD' stands for 'lethal dose'). Using these figures, place the compounds in order of increasing toxicity.

c) Compounds which boil between 40 °C and 70 °C are preferred as they are easy to use in vaporisers. Which compounds listed boil within this range?

d) Which compound is the most satisfactory anaesthetic? Explain your choice.

8 Copy the diagrams and statements. Draw a line to link each description of an organic molecule with the correct structural formula.

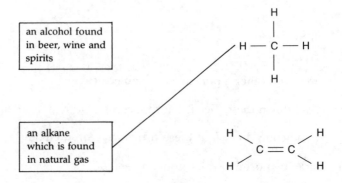

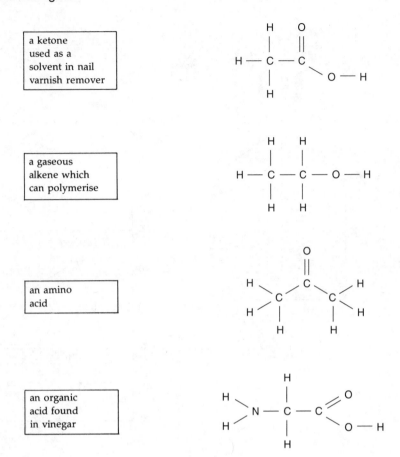

| a ketone used as a solvent in nail varnish remover |
| a gaseous alkene which can polymerise |
| an amino acid |
| an organic acid found in vinegar |

9 A home wine-making kit contains the following items:

1 demijohn (large bottle)
1 airlock
1 heating unit (controlled by a thermostat)
sugar
grape juice
yeast
yeast nutrient
sterilising tablets

The procedure outlined overleaf was followed during the production of one batch of wine.

After sterilising the glassware, the sugar, yeast, yeast nutrient and grape juice were dissolved in water and added to the demijohn. The heater and airlock were fitted, and the demijohn placed in a dark cupboard for eight weeks. During this time, the bubbles of gas coming through the airlock were counted for one minute each day, and the results used to plot the graph.

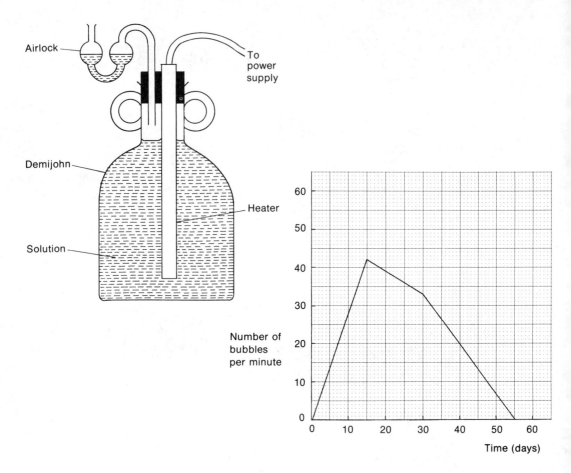

a) Why is it important to sterilise the equipment used in making wine?

b) i)   Name the process in which sugar is converted into ethanol (alcohol) using yeast.

    ii) Which gas is a by-product of this process?

c) i)   Explain why the airlock is necessary.

    ii) Why is it important to prevent the temperature from becoming too high or too low?

d) i)   After how long did the rate of ethanol production reach a maximum?

    ii) When did ethanol production stop?

e) What method would you use to separate ethanol from the solution in the demijohn?

f) 4 moles of ethanol (C_2H_5OH) can be produced from 1 mole of sucrose ($C_{12}H_{22}O_{11}$).

    i)   Calculate the maximum mass of ethanol that could, in theory, be obtained from 342 g sucrose.

    ii) Why is it unlikely that all the sugar will be converted into alcohol?

10 Ethanol, the alcohol present in beer, wine and spirits, can affect a person's ability to drive or operate machinery when present in the bloodstream at levels below the legal limit (80 mg in 100 cm³ blood). The effects of drinking various amounts of alcohol are shown on the next page.

Drinks consumed	Approximate blood alcohol level (mg/100 cm³)	Effects
1 bottle of whisky	500	Death possible
¾ bottle of whisky	400	Unconsciousness, coma possible
6½ pints of beer	200	Loss of memory, double vision, difficulty in walking
5 pints of beer or 10 whiskies	150	Loss of self-control, slurred speech
-------------------------------	80 mg legal limit	-------------------------------
2 pints of beer or 4 whiskies	60	Judgement is markedly impaired
1 pint of beer or 2 glasses of wine	30	Likelihood of an accident begins to increase

The reaction of a person to alcoholic drink depends on several factors, including body mass. In an average individual, the amount of alcohol in the bloodstream will rise gradually for about 1 hour after drinking a pint of beer, then fall to zero after a further 2 hours. The graph below shows the blood alcohol level of a person, from midday to midnight, on a day when he or she consumes alcoholic drinks at lunch time and after leaving work.

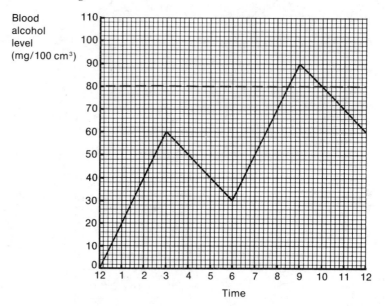

a) Which of the following terms describes the action of ethanol?

   stimulant   depressant   narcotic

b) How many i) single whiskies ii) glasses of wine are equivalent to 1 pint of beer?

c) i) Give two factors, apart from body mass, which will affect a person's response to alcoholic drink.

   ii) Use the information provided to estimate the minimum number of pints of beer needed to raise the amount of alcohol in the bloodstream above the legal limit.

d) Use the graph to answer the following questions:

   i) For how long is the person's blood alcohol level over the legal limit?

   ii) What is the rate of decrease of blood alcohol in mg/100 cm³ blood/hour?

   iii) Someone goes to bed at midnight with a blood alcohol level of 200 mg/100 cm³. Is it likely that his or her blood alcohol level will be below the legal limit when he or she is driving to work at 7.00 a.m.?

e) Which organ in the body breaks down alcohol in the bloodstream?

f) Describe two serious health problems caused by prolonged heavy drinking.

11 Read the following passage and answer the questions which follow.

Before 1856, dyes were obtained from animals, plants and minerals. Woad, a blue dye extracted from a plant of the same name, was used by ancient tribes as a body dye, while the crimson dye cochineal was extracted from crushed insect shells. Lead compounds were used in paint, but this is much less common today. The variety of colours available increased following W.H. Perkin's discovery of **synthetic** 'coal tar' dyes in the nineteenth century.

There are many types of dye in use today, including **mordant dyes** and **reactive dyes**. With mordant dyeing, a piece of cloth is placed in a bath containing a solution of aluminium ions (the mordant). It is then transferred to a second bath which contains hydroxide ions. A precipitate is formed on the fibres of the cloth. When the cloth is added to a solution containing the dye, the coloured material attaches itself to the precipitate. Colours obtained in this way are not particularly **fast**.

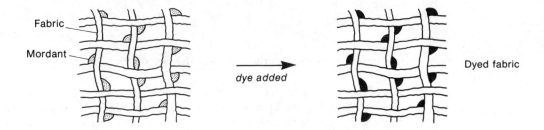

Reactive dyes become attached to the fabric directly. They consist of large molecules which can be drawn in the following simplified way:

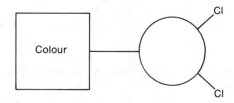

When cloth is dyed, the chlorine atoms in the dye are displaced during a chemical reaction with the cloth. Colours obtained in this way are bright and do not fade with washing.

a)   What is meant by the words 'fast' and 'synthetic' as used in the passage?

b)   Suggest a chemical name for the mordant.

c)   Explain why ammonia solution produces a precipitate with the mordant.

d)   When a reactive dye bonds with a fibre as shown above, what other product is formed?

e)   Explain why cloth coloured with a reactive dye is less likely to fade with washing than one coloured with a mordant dye.

f)   Design a fair test to compare the resistance to fading in light of two identical pieces of red cloth – one coloured with a mordant dye the other with a reactive dye.

12   Read the following passage and then answer the questions.

> Soap can be made by boiling a fat or oil with sodium hydroxide solution. The soap is separated from the reaction mixture by adding a concentrated solution of sodium chloride. This causes the soap to form a solid skin on the surface of the solution. Another product of the reaction is the alcohol glycerol which can be **isolated** using distillation. **Excess** sodium chloride solution is tapped off and **recycled**. After separation, the soap is washed, dried, scented (and coloured if required) before being pressed into tablets.

a)   Use the information provided to draw a flow diagram for the production of soap.

b)   Explain the meaning of the words 'isolated', 'excess' and 'recycled' as used in the passage.

c)   Name one other metal hydroxide which could be used instead of sodium hydroxide to make soap.

d)   In hard water, calcium ions react with soap to form an insoluble compound (scum):

$$2C_{17}H_{35}CO_2Na\,(aq) + Ca^{2+}\,(aq) \longrightarrow (C_{17}H_{35}CO_2)_2Ca\,(s) + 2\,Na^+\,(aq)$$
     soap   calcium ion   scum   sodium ions

   i)   How does the chemical equation show that scum is insoluble?

   ii) Describe one method of removing calcium ions from hard water.

e)   What precautions would you take when making soap on a small scale in the laboratory?

13 A soap or detergent molecule may be thought of as having an electrically charged 'head' which likes water and hates grease or oil, and a hydrocarbon 'tail' which likes grease or oil and hates water.

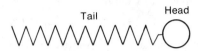

Tail   Head

Use this information to help you to explain each of the following observations.

a) Oil and water do not mix, but when a few drops of detergent are added and the mixture stirred, the oil disperses and a milky sol is formed. The oil remains dispersed if the sol is left to stand.

b) With care, a pin can be made to float on water. If detergent is carefully added, the pin sinks and cannot be refloated.

c) Water droplets do not soak in quickly with some types of cloth, but detergent solution is quickly absorbed.

d) Greasy clothes can be cleaned more efficiently by agitating in detergent solution; water alone has little effect.

14 Washing powders are complex mixtures. One type, Serpil, contains the following ingredients:

> detergent and soap
> enzymes
> bleach
> sodium phosphate
> perfume

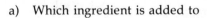

a) Which ingredient is added to

   i) give the clothes a pleasant smell

   ii) improve the wetting power of water, and to remove grease stains

   iii) remove stains such as egg yolk and blood in a low temperature (30–40 °C) soak?

b) An advertisement for Serpil states that the powder 'digests dirt and stains'. Is this a fair claim? Explain your answer.

c) The bleach works at high temperatures only. What problems would be caused by using a more powerful bleach which works at all temperatures?

d) Sodium phosphate removes the hardness in water. Why is soft water better for washing purposes?

e) Washing powders can be a source of pollution. If some washing water contaminated a pond, what effect would the following ingredients have on the organisms listed, and why?

Ingredient	*Organism*
i) sodium phosphate	pond-weed
ii) detergent	pond-skater (an insect which walks on the surface of the water)

15 a) What causes hardness in water?

b) What is the difference between temporary and permanent hardness?

c) Describe and explain one method for removing each type of hardness.

d) List two problems which occur in household appliances due to hard water.

16 Copy and complete the following table, which describes types of colloid.

Type of colloid	Dispersion medium	Disperse phase	Example (s)
Solid gel	Solid	Solid	
Solid emulsion	Solid		Butter
	Solid	Gas	Meringue
Paste	Liquid	Solid	
Emulsion	Liquid		Milk
Foam		Gas	
	Gas	Solid	Smoke
Aerosol			Cloud

17 The list below gives pairs of words used to describe materials. Choose one word from each pair to describe the materials listed.

        strong/weak   brittle/elastic   biodegradable/rot-proof
        transparent/opaque   electrical conductor/insulator

Materials:

a)   rubber

b)   glass

c)   iron

d)   bakelite (thermosetting plastic)

e)   carbon (graphite)

f)   polyvinyl chloride (PVC)

18 A student prepared a sample of lead borate glass using the following method.

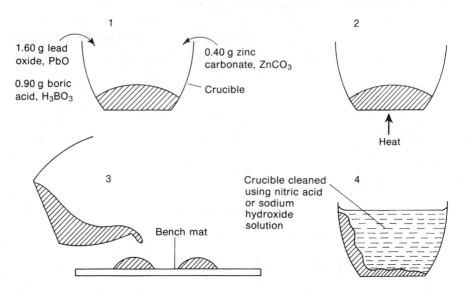

a) i)   Calculate the percentage by mass of lead oxide in the initial mixture.

ii) What precaution must be taken after working with the ingredients in this experiment?

b) What is the name of the gas produced when zinc carbonate is heated? Write a word equation for the decomposition.

c) Would lead borate glass be useful for making test tubes? Explain your answer.

d) One of the glass beads cracked and split into two pieces while cooling. Copy and complete the following explanation by choosing the correct word from the brackets:

When a glass bead solidifies on the bench mat, the (inside/outside) cools more quickly, and begins to (expand/contract). This produces strains in the surface of the glass, which is weak under (compression/tension), and can lead to cracks which split the bead. To prevent this from happening, the glass should be cooled very (quickly/slowly) in a process called (quenching/annealing).

e) Traces of other metal oxides can be added to the melt to produce coloured glass. Which of the following oxides are likely to have this effect, and why?

potassium oxide   manganese oxide   copper oxide
magnesium oxide   cobalt oxide

f) The structures of boron oxide and lead borate glass are shown opposite.

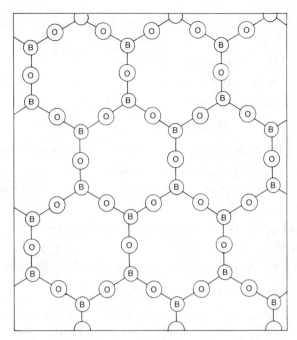

Crystalline boron oxide consists of chains of triangular units containing boron and oxygen atoms

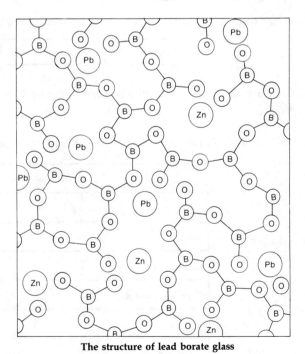

The structure of lead borate glass

i)   Study the diagrams, then write down two similarities and two differences between the structures.

ii) Which substance, boron oxide or lead borate glass, has the higher melting point? Give reasons for your answer.

19 A sample of soda-lime glass is made by heating a mixture with the following composition.

 sodium carbonate (Na_2CO_3) 15%
 silicon dioxide (SiO_2) 75%
 calcium carbonate $(CaCO_3)$ 10%

a) List the elements present in soda-lime glass.

b) What mass of each ingredient must be taken to make 50 g of reaction mixture?

c) After heating, the mixture contains silicon dioxide together with oxides of sodium and calcium. What benefit is there in having metal oxides present in the melt?

d) List four household items made from glass. Is the type of glass the same for each object?

e) Why are drinking glasses manufactured with different compositions?

f) Here are some properties of glass:

 hard   resistant to chemicals   easily cleaned   heat resistant transparent   brittle   breaks up into sharp fragments poor conductor of heat

Arrange these properties under two headings as shown below:

Advantages	Disadvantages

g) Make a list of four ways in which recycling glass saves energy.

20 The following table shows the typical composition of car exhaust fumes.

Gas	Abundance (%)
Nitrogen	68
Water	10
Carbon dioxide	9
Carbon monoxide	8
Oxygen	3
Hydrogen	1
Hydrocarbon fuel	0.5
Nitrogen oxides	0.5

a) i) Which gas, present in the mixture, is needed to burn petrol?

   ii) Explain why this gas is present in the exhaust mixture.

b) Explain how both carbon dioxide and carbon monoxide are formed when petrol burns in a car engine.

c) Which gases, present in the exhaust mixture, can cause

   i) acid rain?

   ii) global warming?

3 THE CHEMISTRY OF LIFE

Food and Food Tests

1   Carbohydrates, fats and proteins are important classes of compounds found in living organisms.

Copy and complete this table by placing a tick under each element that is found in the foods given:

	Carbon	Hydrogen	Oxygen	Nitrogen
Carbohydrate				
Protein				
Fat				

2   Copy and complete these sentences about **proteins**:

a)   Proteins are made up of smaller units called _____.

b)   About _____ different amino acids occur in nature.

c)   Small chains of amino acids are called _____.

d)   Some proteins are tough and fibre-like, forming structures such as hair, _____ and _____.

e)   Substances called _____ are proteins that control the rate of chemical reactions in the body.

3   A student placed some breadcrumbs in a test tube, added an equal amount of copper (II) oxide powder, and mixed the contents. A delivery bend was fitted and the tube and contents were heated. A second test tube of limewater (calcium hydroxide solution) was held just below the delivery bend.

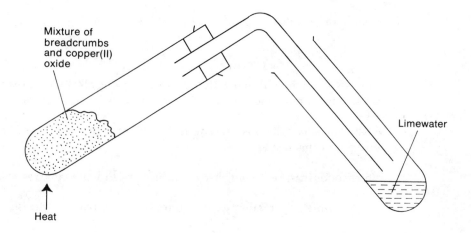

After a few minutes, droplets of a colourless liquid were seen in the delivery bend, and the limewater turned cloudy near the surface. The colourless liquid turned anhydrous copper (II) sulphate from white to blue.

a)   What liquid was present in the delivery bend?

b)   How could you show that the liquid was pure?

c)   Name the gas produced in this test which turns limewater milky.

d)   Explain how these results demonstrate that carbon and hydrogen are present in the substances contained in breadcrumbs.

e)   Explain why it is not possible to conclude that oxygen is present in the substances contained in breadcrumbs.

f)   What is a **carbohydrate**?

4   Copy and complete the following table by giving details about tests for glucose and starch.

	Glucose	*Starch*
What is the testing reagent?		
How much reagent is needed to test 2 cm^3 of solution?		
Is heat required?		
What is the colour of a positive test?		

5   A test for proteins is the **biuret test**.

a)   Which two reagents are used in this test?

b)   Describe how you would use them to test 2 cm^3 of a solution for protein.

c)   What is the result of a positive test?

6   a)   Milk powder, when heated with soda lime (a strong alkali), releases a gas which turns moist litmus paper blue. What is the likely identity of the gas?

b)   What substance which is present in the milk powder could act as a source of nitrogen in this test?

c)   Which foods in the following list would also produce the same result in this test?

   egg white   **margarine**   **glucose**   **starch**   **cheese**

7   Use the information in the table below to identify the types of food (protein, starch, sugar) present in each of the foods A, B and C.

Food	Result of adding sodium hydroxide and copper sulphate solutions	Result of adding iodine solution	Result of heating with Benedict's solution
A	Purple colour	Brown colour	Blue colour
B	Blue colour	Black colour	Orange colour
C	Purple colour	Brown colour	Blue colour

a)   A contains _____.

b)   B contains _____.

c)   C contains _____.

8   A pupil was given five powders A, B, C, D and E. Each powder was dissolved in water and tested for the presence of

>   **Glucose – using Benedict's test**
>   **Starch – using the iodine test**
>   **Protein – using the biuret test**

The table of results below shows the final colour observed at the end of each of the tests.

	Powder A	Powder B	Powder C	Powder D	Powder E
Benedict's test	Orange	Blue	Blue	Orange	Blue
Iodine test	Black	Black	Yellow/brown	Black	Yellow/brown
Biuret test	Blue	Blue	Purple	Purple	Blue

Which powder contained

a)   protein only

b)   starch only

c)   starch and glucose only

d)   glucose, starch and protein

e)   none of these substances?

9   Below are shown parts of two molecules of fat.

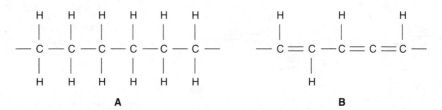

   A   B

a)   What kind of fat is shown by each of molecules A and B?

b)   Explain your answer to a) for molecule B.

c)   What kind of food material is each fat molecule *more likely* to have come from?

d)   What advice would you give to someone about the relative amounts of A and B they should include in their diet?

e)   Explain the reasons for your advice.

10   The label on a snack food gave the following information:

This product does not contain any artificial colours, sweeteners or presevatives.	
Nutritional Information (per 100 g)	
FAT	14.5 g
PROTEIN	29.9 g
CARBOHYDRATE	52.5 g
FIBRE	2.2 g

a)   Which three elements are found in carbohydrates, and in what ratio?

b)   Which of the nutrients listed contains the most nitrogen?

c)   Which of the nutrients listed would provide the most energy per gram?

d)   What *types* of small molecule would be produced when the following are digested?

   i)   protein

   ii)   carbohydrate

Digestion

1   This diagram shows how carbohydrates are interchangeable.

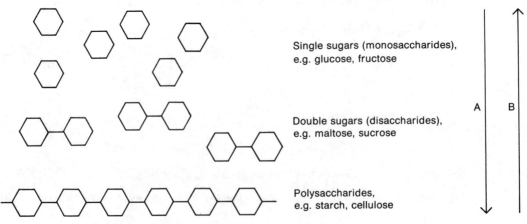

a)   Copy the diagram.

b)   What type of reaction is represented by arrow A on the diagram?

c)   What type of reaction is represented by arrow B on the diagram?

2   The following results were obtained from an experiment in which saliva was mixed
with a starch suspension. Samples of the mixture were kept in water baths at
different temperatures for 15 minutes. At the end of this time the samples were
analysed to find out how much sugar has been produced in each. The results are
given below.

Temperature (°C)	0	10	20	30	40	50	60	70	80
Units of sugar	12	36	65	90	90	60	30	4	2

a)   Plot a graph of these results drawing a smooth curve through the points. Label
the axes as shown.

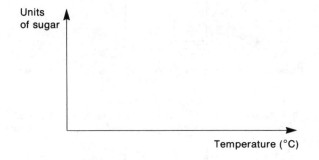

b)   What kind of substance must be present in the saliva to break down the starch
into sugar?

c)   At which temperatures is most sugar produced?

d)   Why is very little sugar formed when the saliva and starch mixture are kept at a
high temperature?

e)   What other factors, besides temperature, would affect the amount of sugar
produced from a starch and saliva mixture?

f)   Can saliva break down any substances other than starch? Explain your answer.

3   The diagrams below show the main stages of an investigation into the digestion of milk fat by a lipase. Phenol red was used to indicate changes in the pH of the contents of the tubes. Phenol red is pink in alkaline solution and yellow in acid solution. The investigation was carried out at room temperature.

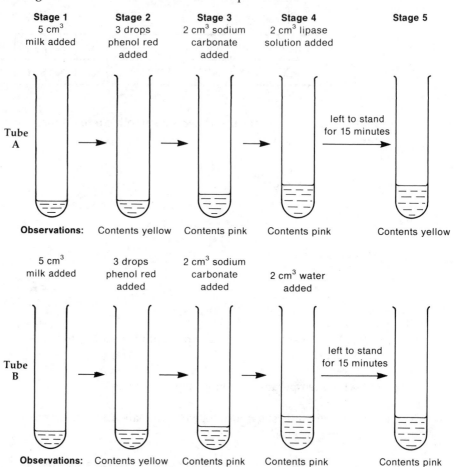

a)   Why was the sodium carbonate added at stage 3?

b)   Why was only water added to tube B at stage 4?

c)   What has happened in tube A to produce the change in pH from stages 4 to 5? Explain your answer fully.

d)   Where does the digestion of fats by enzymes begin in the human body?

e)   What else is necessary in the gut besides enzymes to start the digestion of fats?

f)   What role does it play?

g)   Why is it not necessary to add it to the digestion mixture in this experiment?

h)   Why is this particular experiment unsuitable for determining the effect of pH on the activity of the lipase?

4 The diagram below shows an experiment to investigate the effect of salivary amylase on starch at different temperatures.

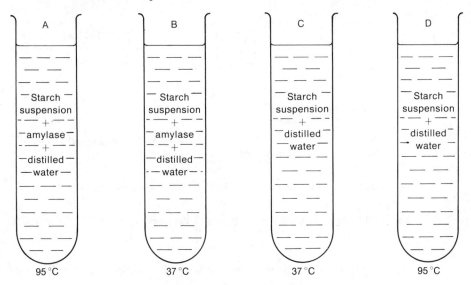

After 30 minutes each tube was tested for the presence of **reducing sugars**.

a) In which tube(s) would you expect a positive result?

b) Explain the reasoning for your answer to a).

5 Look up the information required to complete the table below which shows some uses of enzymes. Copy and complete the table.

Use	Enzyme involved	Explanation
Washing clothes	Proteases	Biological washing powders dissolve protein stains e.g. blood.
Tenderising meat	Proteases	
Making syrup and fruit juice		Starch is broken down into sweet sugars.
	Cellulase	The tough cellulose cell walls are broken down.
Cheese making	Rennin	

6 The diagram below represents two amino acids joined together in part of a protein chain.

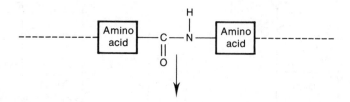

a) Copy and complete the equation to show what happens if the bond between the amino acids is hydrolysed.

b) Name the type of enzyme that would speed up this reaction.

c) State *one* other way which could be used to speed up the reaction, besides enzyme action.

d) Where would this reaction first take place in the human digestive system?

e) Use the equation to explain why the *joining together* of amino acids into a protein chain is called 'condensation polymerisation'.

7 The diagram below represents a protein molecule.

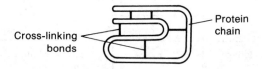

a) Draw the molecule as it might look after being denatured.

b) Explain what happens to a protein molecule when it is denatured.

c) The protein albumen in egg white can be denatured by whisking (beating). State *one* other way of denaturing a protein.

8 Below is a graph showing how enzyme activity changes with temperature.

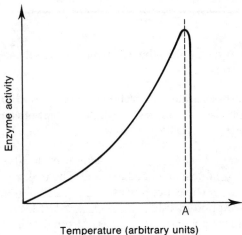

a) For most mammalian enzymes, what is the temperature at A?

b) Explain the shape of the graph.

c) Use the graph to explain how food is preserved by refrigeration.

d) In order to store vegetables such as carrots for long periods, they are first 'blanched' (boiled for a few seconds) and then deep frozen. Use the graph above to explain how this method works.

e) Which of the graphs below shows the way in which enzyme activity changes with pH?

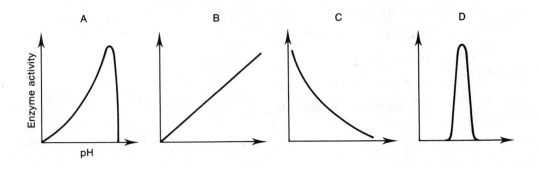

Photosynthesis and Respiration

1 a) Copy and complete the following passage choosing words from this list to fill in the blanks:

> carbohydrate   carbon dioxide   chlorophyll   complicated
> glucose   leaves   light   photosynthesis   oxygen   small
> Sun   waste   water

Green plants take in _____ simple molecules and convert them into the large _____ ones they need for food. The making of food by green plants is called _____. The process uses _____ energy from the _____. The energy is trapped by the _____ in the leaves. Two simple raw materials are involved in the process, _____ from the air and _____ from the soil. It takes place mainly in the _____ of the plant. The most common kind of food produced is _____ which is a _____. The gas _____ is a _____ product of the process.

b) Why is this process which takes place in green plants called *photo*synthesis?

2 Plants use the sugars that they make by photosynthesis to make all the other large complicated molecules that they need. Here are some examples:

> amino acids   cellulose   chlorophyll   starch

Which of these examples

a) is needed to make cell walls

b) acts as a food store

c) are needed to make proteins

d) is contained in chloroplasts?

3 Some of the glucose made by photosynthesis is oxidised in respiration to provide energy for the plant.

a) Write down an equation for the oxidation of glucose in respiration in either words or symbols.

b) Describe two activities for which a plant needs the energy from respiration.

4 INDUSTRIAL PROCESSES

Extraction of Raw Materials

1 Crude oil is an example of a fossil fuel. At an oil refinery, it is cleaned then separated into fractions by fractional distillation. Part of the fractionating column is drawn below.

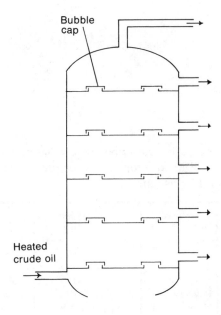

a) What is a fossil fuel? Name two other fossil fuels.

b) Explain how a fractionating column separates crude oil into fractions, referring to the diagram in your answer.

c) Arrange the following fractions in order of increasing boiling point.

  LPG   kerosine   naphtha   heavy oil

d) Write down a major use for any *two* of the above fractions.

e) Explain what is meant by the description of fossil fuels as **non-renewable** energy sources.

2 The diagram below shows a simplified diagram of a distillation tower at an oil refinery.

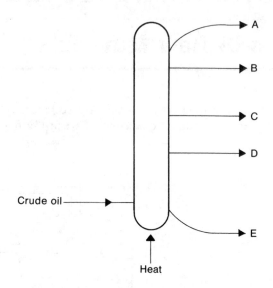

a) Each of the fractions described below was obtained from the tower at one of the positions A–E. Make a copy of the diagram and at each position name the correct fraction and its use(s).

Name	Boiling point range (°C)	Use
Kerosine	160–250	Jet fuel
Gasoline	40–180	Car fuel, raw material (plastics)
Diesel oil	220–340	Fuel for diesel engines
Refinery gas	40 and below	Camping gas
Heavy gas oil	350 and above	Fuel oil, tar for roads

b) There are a number of 'bubble caps' inside the tower at various levels, through which the vapour must pass during distillation.

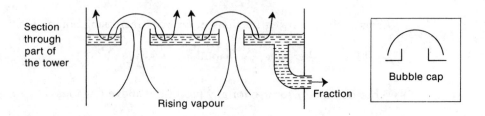

Explain how bubble caps help to separate fractions in the tower.

3 Find out about the Frasch process for extracting sulphur. Draw a diagram of the equipment used, explain how it works, and give two important industrial uses for the sulphur obtained.

4 The following table gives information on a family of organic compounds called **alkanes**. They are found in crude oil.

Name of alkane	Boiling point (°C)	Physical state at room temperature	Number of carbon atoms per molecule
Methane	−160	gas	1
Propane	−40	gas	3
Butane	1		
Pentane	35	liquid	
Heptane	160	liquid	7

a) What physical state would you expect for butane at room temperature (25 °C)?

b) i) Plot a graph of boiling point (y-axis) against number of carbon atoms (x-axis) for the three alkanes methane, propane and heptane.

  ii) Use your graph to find the number of carbon atoms in a molecule of butane.

c) Give the molecular formula and structural formula for methane.

d) Write a balanced chemical equation for the complete combustion of methane.

Inorganic Processes

1 Lead is found in the ground as the ore **galena**.

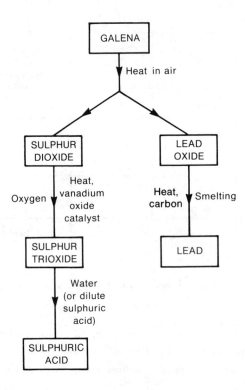

The above process shows how sulphuric acid and lead are made from galena.

a) Which two elements are present in galena?

b) Write a word equation for the formation of sulphur trioxide in this process.

c) Name a metal other than lead which can be extracted from its ore by smelting.

d) Complete the equation below, which shows the reaction between lead oxide and carbon:

   $PbO + C \longrightarrow$

2 Copy and complete the following sentences, which concern the Haber process for making ammonia.

a) The raw materials for the Haber process are _____.

b) Nitrogen and hydrogen are fed into the ammonia converter in the ratio _____.

c) The catalyst in the ammonia converter is _____.

d) Ammonia can be removed from the gases leaving the converter by _____.

e) Unconverted nitrogen and hydrogen are _____.

f) The formula of ammonia is _____.

g) Two important industrial uses of ammonia are _____.

3 In the **contact process**, sulphuric acid is manufactured from sulphur in several stages. Firstly, purified molten sulphur is fed into a furnace where it burns in air to produce sulphur dioxide. This gas is then oxidised further to sulphur trioxide, using vanadium pentoxide catalyst. When sulphur trioxide is absorbed in pre-prepared sulphuric acid, oleum is produced. Finally, oleum is diluted with water to produce more sulphuric acid than was present originally.

a) Using the information supplied, copy and complete the flowchart for the contact process.

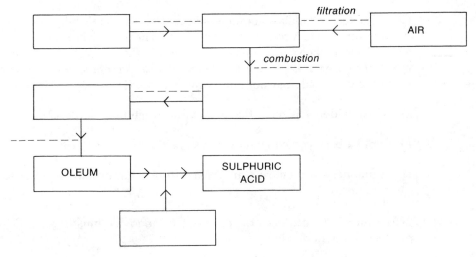

b) What are the formulae of the two oxides of sulphur?

c) Explain why the conversions

sulphur $\longrightarrow$ sulphur dioxide
sulphur dioxide $\longrightarrow$ sulphur trioxide
are oxidation reactions.

d) i)   Describe two dangers arising from a leak of sulphur dioxide from the converter, one local and one global.

ii)   Name another source of sulphur dioxide pollution.

e)   Sulphuric acid is required for a number of important chemical processes. Name two materials which require sulphuric acid for their production.

4   Nitric acid manufacture involves the catalytic oxidation of ammonia.

$$NH_3\,(g) + O_2\,(g) \xrightarrow[\text{catalyst}]{\text{platinum–rhodium}} NO + H_2O$$

This process was carried out in the laboratory using the following apparatus.

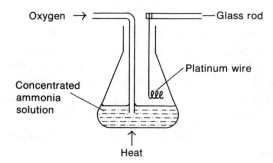

Concentrated ammonia solution was heated very gently while a stream of oxygen bubbled through it. A coil of platinum wire was heated in a Bunsen flame to red heat, allowed to cool then suspended over the solution as shown. The wire began to glow again. The experiment can be dangerous as ammonia will sometimes burn explosively in a side reaction under these conditions.

a)   What evidence is there that a chemical reaction took place?

b)   Write a balanced equation for this reaction.

c)   Ammonia will not burn in air. What feature of this experiment leads to ammonia combustion?

Before nitric acid can be formed, nitrogen monoxide must react with oxygen to produce nitrogen dioxide.

$$NO\,(g) + O_2\,(g) \longrightarrow NO_2\,(g)$$

d)   Suggest a source of oxygen for this reaction.

e)   Write a balanced equation for the reaction between NO and O_2.

f)   Give one large-scale use of nitric acid.

5 The cycle of reactions shows how three substances, calcium carbonate, calcium oxide and calcium hydroxide, can be interconverted.

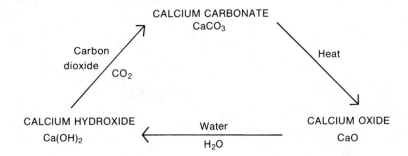

a) Name one form of calcium carbonate which is found as rock.

b) Name the gas produced when calcium carbonate is heated.

c) i) What happens when calcium carbonate is added to water?
   ii) What happens when calcium carbonate is added to dilute hydrochloric acid?

d) Describe one use of calcium carbonate in industry.

e) Suggest a method for converting calcium hydroxide into calcium oxide.

f) Describe how calcium hydroxide solution can be used to test for carbon dioxide. Write a word equation for the reaction which takes place when such a test is positive.

g) Write a few sentences about the use of calcium hydroxide in any *three* of the following applications:

   i) water purification, including effluent treatment
   ii) agriculture
   iii) steel production
   iv) tanning

6   The following diagram shows a **blast furnace**, which is used to extract iron from iron
ore:

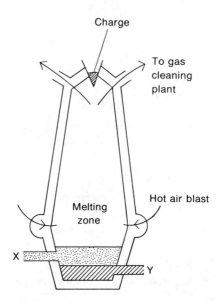

a)   What are the three ingredients in the charge?

b)   At which point (X or Y) is iron tapped off?

c)   Balance the following equation for the reduction of iron ore to iron:

$$Fe_2O_3(s) + CO(g) \longrightarrow Fe(l) + CO_2(g)$$

d)   The iron extracted from the furnace (pig iron) is very brittle and melts below the
melting point of pure iron. Why is this?

e)   Name two impurities present in pig iron.

f)   Give two reasons for preventing the escape of the waste gases.

g)   Hydrogen will reduce iron ore to iron. Why is this method not used on a large
scale?

7 The diagram below shows how iron produced in a blast furnace is converted to steel.

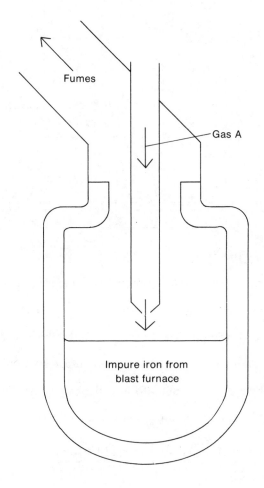

a) Name gas A.

b) i) One impurity present in the iron is carbon. Name one gas (other than gas A) which will be present in the fumes.

   ii) Name one other impurity present in the iron from a blast furnace.

c) i) Which non-metal is present in steel?

   ii) Name one metallic element that may be added to the iron during its conversion to steel.

8   Aluminium is extracted from its ore, bauxite (Al_2O_3) using electrolytic reduction in steel-walled cells as shown below.

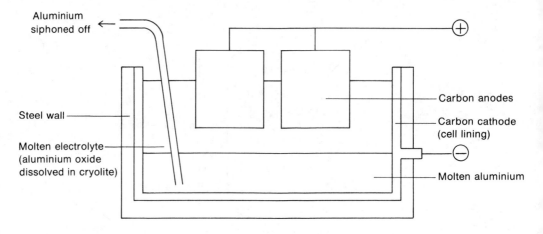

a)   Copy the diagram.

b)   What must be done to the bauxite before it is added to the cell?

c)   Why is aluminium not extracted in a blast furnace?

d)   What is the purpose of the cryolite in this process?

e)   Explain why the anodes must be replaced regularly.

f)   Why is there no need to heat the cell externally during electrolysis?

g)   Balance the equations for the change occurring at each electrode:

   i)   Anode $\boxed{}$ O^{2-} $\longrightarrow$ $O_2 +$ $\boxed{}$ e^-

   ii)   Cathode $Al^{3+} +$ $\boxed{}$ $e^- \longrightarrow$ Al (e^- = an electron)

h)   Explain why aluminium extraction plants are frequently sited close to hydro-electric power stations.

i)   Give *three* uses of aluminium.

9   The following experiment models an industrial process (electrolysis) used to obtain several useful products from sodium chloride and water.

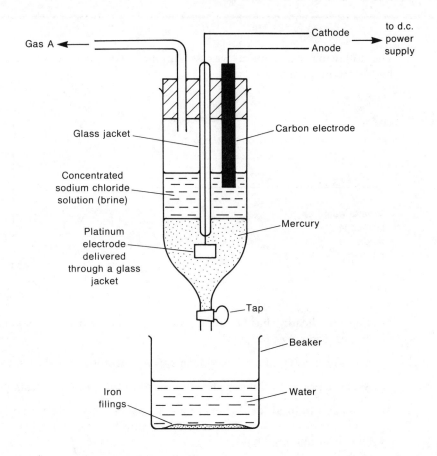

a)   During the electrolysis, the gas A produced is found to bleach moist litmus paper. Suggest a name for gas A.

b)   After 10 minutes, the power is switched off, and the tap opened to allow the mercury to run through into the beaker of water. A flammable gas, B, is produced, which burns with a squeaky pop. The water becomes strongly alkaline.

   i)   Suggest a name for gas B.

   ii) Suggest a name for the alkaline solution.

c)   Explain why the platinum electrode is delivered to the mercury in a glass jacket.

d)   If the experiment is repeated with no iron filings, very little gas B is produced. Suggest a reason for including iron filings in the beaker of water.

Organic Processes

1   The following experiment was set up to carry out catalytic cracking of the hydrocarbon, paraffin:

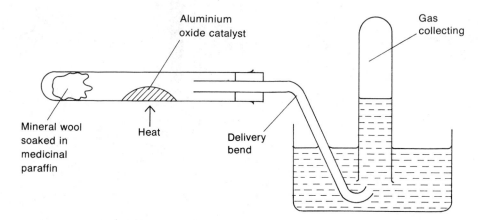

a)   Once the heating has begun, it must not be stopped while the delivery bend is under water. Why is this?

b)   Paraffin is a liquid alkane. Which gaseous alkane is used as a domestic fuel?

c)   What happens to the paraffin molecules in the process of catalytic cracking?

d)   The paraffin used for this experiment was tested with bromine (in an organic solvent), together with the gas collected during the experiment. The results are shown in the table below:

Substance tested	Effect on bromine solution
Medicinal paraffin	No effect (remains orange/brown)
Gases collected during catalytic cracking	Bromine decolorised (turns colourless and clear)

What type of hydrocarbon must be present among the gases collected?

e)   Choose from the following list the correct description of the reaction between ethene and bromine:

neutralisation   addition   substitution   dehydration

f)   Why is catalytic cracking necessary on an industrial scale?

g)   The products of catalytic cracking undergo polymerisation. Describe what happens to the molecules in this process.

h)   What important type of material is produced in polymerisation?

2 a) A part of crude oil used to make plastics is called naphtha. It contains **saturated hydrocarbons** with between 8 and 12 carbon atoms in each molecule.

    i) Explain the meaning of the words 'saturated' and 'hydrocarbon'.

    ii) Copy the flow diagram below which shows how naphtha is converted to plastics. Name processes 1 and 2 on your diagram.

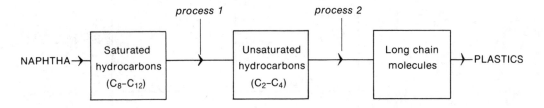

b) Copy and complete the table comparing fractional distillation of crude oil in the laboratory with industrial fractionation of crude oil.

Industrial fractionation	Laboratory fractional distillation
	Batch process
Separation improved using bubble caps	
	Fractions are taken from the top of the column

3 a) Copy and complete the following table, which shows additional polymerisation products from molecules based on ethene.

Monomer	Polymer
H$\quad$H \\$\quad\quad$/ $\quad$C $=$ C /$\quad\quad$\\ H$\quad\quad$H **Ethene**	$\left[\begin{array}{c}\text{H}\quad\text{H} \\ \mid\quad\mid \\ \text{C}-\text{C} \\ \mid\quad\mid \\ \text{H}\quad\text{H}\end{array}\right]_n$ **Polythene**
Cl$\quad\quad$H \\$\quad\quad$/ $\quad$C $=$ C /$\quad\quad$\\ H$\quad\quad$H **Vinyl chloride**	**Polyvinyl chloride**
	$\left[\begin{array}{c}\text{H}\quad\text{C}_6\text{H}_5 \\ \mid\quad\mid \\ \text{C}-\text{C} \\ \mid\quad\mid \\ \text{H}\quad\text{H}\end{array}\right]_n$ **Polystyrene**
Styrene	
F$\quad\quad$F \\$\quad\quad$/ $\quad$C $=$ C /$\quad\quad$\\ F$\quad\quad$F **Teflon monomer**	**Teflon**
	$\left[\begin{array}{c}\text{H}\quad\text{CH}_3 \\ \mid\quad\mid \\ \text{C}-\text{C} \\ \mid\quad\mid \\ \text{H}\quad\text{H}\end{array}\right]_n$ **Polypropene**
Propene	

b) Name one polymer made by the process of condensation polymerisation, and explain how this process gets its name.

c) Explain why chemists produce such a variety of monomers.

4   The economics of some forming processes for the manufacture of plastic articles are compared in the table below.

Process	Cost of machinery	Speed of the process	Problems with the process
Compression moulding	Moderate	Slow	Excess material needs trimming
Injection moulding	High	Fast	Split mould gives joint lines on product
Vacuum forming	Low	Slow	Uneven thickness

a)   Small ice-cream tubs could be made by injection moulding or vacuum forming. Which method would you choose, and why?

b)   Suggest a thermosoftening plastic which would be suitable for making ice-cream tubs.

c)   Compression moulding is often used to produce plastic door handles and electrical switch housings. Which type of plastic – thermosoftening or thermo-setting – would best suit these applications? Explain your choice.

d)   Which method would be most suitable for mass-producing nylon combs? Explain your choice.

e)   The forming methods above are all **batch** processes, while extrusion is a **continuous** process. Explain the meaning of the words 'batch' and 'continuous' as used here.

5   Ethene, C_2H_4, an important raw material in the plastics industry, can be made by dehydrating ethanol, C_2H_5OH.

a)   Write a balanced chemical equation for the dehydration of ethanol.

b)   Draw a diagram of the apparatus you would use to carry out this reaction and collect the gaseous product.

c)   What could be used to catalyse the dehydration?

d)   Describe a simple chemical test which you could carry out to show that ethene was present after the reaction. Say what you would expect to happen in a positive result.

e)   What happens to the ethene molecules when they polymerise to form polyethene?

5 CHEMICAL CALCULATIONS

Chemical Equations

1   Which of the following accurately describes the information given in the equation below?

$$2HgO \longrightarrow 2Hg + O_2$$

(Hg = mercury, O = oxygen)

A.   2 atoms of mercury oxide form 2 atoms of mercury and 1 atom of oxygen.
B.   2 atoms of mercury oxide form 2 atoms of mercury and 1 molecule of oxygen.
C.   2 molecules of mercury oxide form 2 atoms of mercury and 1 molecule of oxygen.
D.   2 molecules of mercury oxide form 2 molecules of mercury and 1 atom of oxygen.
E.   2 molecules of mercury oxide form 2 molecules of mercury and 1 molecule of oxygen.

2   Write balanced chemical equations for the following industrial processes.

a)   The action of heat on calcium carbonate in the extraction of iron in a blast furnace.

calcium carbonate ($CaCO_3$) $\longrightarrow$ calcium oxide (CaO) + carbon dioxide (CO_2)

b)   The conversion of sulphur dioxide into sulphur trioxide in the contact process for sulphuric acid manufacture.

sulphur dioxide (SO_2) + oxygen (O_2) $\longrightarrow$ sulphur trioxide (SO_3)

c)   The production of ammonia in the Haber process.

nitrogen (N_2) + hydrogen (H_2) $\longrightarrow$ ammonia (NH_3)

d)   The catalytic cracking of octane.

octane (C_8H_{18}) $\longrightarrow$ propene (C_3H_6) + ethene (C_2H_4) + methane (CH_4)

e)   The catalytic oxidation of ammonia during nitric acid manufacture.

ammonia (NH_3) + oxygen (O_2) $\longrightarrow$ nitrogen monoxide (NO) + water (H_2O)

3 Write balanced ionic equations for the following reactions:

a) An emulsion of silver bromide, on standing in light, produces a small amount of metallic silver when silver ions gain an electron.

b) When solutions of sodium bromide and silver nitrate are mixed, a precipitate of silver bromide is formed.

c) When chlorine is bubbled through a solution of sodium bromide, bromine is produced.

The Mole

1 Define the following terms:

a) Avogadro's number

b) 1 mole

c) relative atomic mass

2 What is the mass of:

a) 1 mole of potassium atoms

b) 10 moles of carbon atoms

c) 0.5 moles of silver atoms

d) 2 moles of uranium atoms

e) 0.001 mole of nitrogen atoms?

(Relative atomic masses: $C = 12$, $N = 14$, $K = 39$, $Ag = 107$, $U = 238$)

3 How many moles of each element are present in:

a) 24 g carbon?

b) 5.6 g iron?

c) 4.14 g lead?

d) 1.92 g copper?

(Relative atomic masses: $C = 12$, $Fe = 56$, $Cu = 64$, $Pb = 207$)

4 How many particles are there in each of the following?

    a)   16 g oxygen gas (molecules)

    b)   24 g carbon (atoms)

    c)   390 g potassium (atoms)

    d)   1.8 g water (molecules)

    (Relative atomic masses: H = 1, C = 12, O = 16, K = 39. Avogadro constant: 6.02×10^{23}/mole)

5 Calculate the relative molecular masses of the following substances:

    a)   hydrogen, H_2

    b)   ammonia, NH_3

    c)   sulphur dioxide, SO_2

    d)   octane, C_8H_{18}

    e)   phosphoric acid, H_3PO_4

    (Relative atomic masses: H = 1, C = 12, N = 14, O = 16, P = 31, S = 32)

6 Calculate the percentage by mass of nitrogen in the following fertilisers:

    a)   ammonium nitrate, $NH_4 NO_3$

    b)   ammonium sulphate, $(NH_4)_2 SO_4$

    c)   ammonium phosphate, $(NH_4)_3 PO_4$

    d)   urea, CON_2H_4

    e)   potassium nitrate, KNO_3

    (Relative atomic masses: H = 1, C = 12, N = 14, O = 16, P = 31, S = 32, K = 39)

7 1.8 g magnesium was placed in a crucible and heated strongly. The heating was continued until no further change took place. After cooling, the contents of the crucible weighed 3.0 g.

    a)   How many moles of magnesium were used?

    b)   What mass of oxygen combined with the magnesium during the experiment?

    c)   How many moles of oxygen combined with the magnesium?

    d)   How many moles of oxygen would react exactly with 1 mole of magnesium?

    e)   What is the formula of magnesium oxide?

    (Relative atomic masses: Mg = 24, O = 16)

8 A mixture of copper and sulphur powders reacts when heated. A hard glass test tube was weighed. A sample of powdered copper was placed inside and the tube was re-weighed. A large excess of sulphur was then added and the contents mixed thoroughly. The tube was then heated strongly until no further change occurred. After cooling the tube was weighed again. A dark blue solid had formed. Readings taken during the experiment are listed below.

Mass of hard glass test tube	16.20 g
Mass of test tube plus copper	16.72 g
Mass of test tube plus compound	16.98 g

a) Describe the appearance of copper and sulphur powders.

b) Give one piece of evidence that a new compound has been formed.

c) What mass of copper was used in the experiment?

d) Explain why it was not necessary to record the mass of sulphur added prior to the reaction.

e) What mass of sulphur combined with the copper?

f) Calculate the number of moles of copper used.

g) Calculate the number of moles of sulphur which reacted.

h) What is the empirical formula of the compound formed?

(Relative atomic masses: $S = 32$, $Cu = 64$)

9 An oxide of iron contains 22.2% oxygen by mass.

a) How many grams of

i)   iron

ii) oxygen

are present in 100 g of the oxide?

b) Calculate the number of moles of each element in 100 g of the oxide.

c) What is the empirical formula of the iron oxide?

(Relative atomic masses: $O = 16$, $Fe = 56$)

10 Iron can be obtained from iron(III) oxide using carbon monoxide according to the
following equation:

$$Fe_2O_3(s) + 3CO(g) \xrightarrow{\text{HEAT}} 2Fe(l) + 2CO_2(g)$$

a) i)   Calculate the mass of 1 mole of iron(III) oxide.

   ii) How many moles of iron can be obtained from 1 mole iron(III) oxide?

b) What mass of iron can be obtained from

   i)   16.0 g iron(III) oxide?

   ii) 4 tonnes iron(III) oxide? (1 tonne $=$ 1000 kg)

c) What mass of carbon dioxide is released for every tonne of iron produced?

(Relative atomic masses: C $=$ 12, O $=$ 16, Fe $=$ 56)

11 The equation below shows how glucose is produced from carbon dioxide and water
during photosynthesis.

$$6CO_2(g) + 6H_2O(g) \xrightarrow{\text{light}} C_6H_{12}O_6(aq) + 6O_2(g)$$

a) What is the relative molecular mass of

   i)   carbon dioxide?

   ii) glucose?

b) How many moles of carbon dioxide are needed to make one mole of glucose?

c) What mass of glucose can be made from 22 g carbon dioxide?

d) What mass of carbon dioxide is needed to make 36 g glucose?

(Relative atomic masses: H $=$ 1, C $=$ 12, O $=$ 16)

12 A sample of glass has the following composition:

   silicon dioxide (SiO_2)   160 g
   sodium oxide (Na_2O)   31 g
   calcium oxide (CaO)   12 g

a) How many moles of silicon dioxide are present in the glass?

b) How many moles of sodium oxide are present in the glass?

c) Find the ratio of silicon atoms to sodium ions in the glass.

(Relative atomic masses: O $=$ 16, Na $=$ 23, Si $=$ 28, Ca $=$ 40)

13 Naturally occurring chlorine (in compounds) consists of 75% of the isotope $^{35}_{17}Cl$ and 25% of the isotope $^{37}_{17}Cl$.

   a) If the atomic number of chlorine is 17, how many electrons are then in an atom of isotope

   i) $^{35}_{17}Cl$?

   ii) $^{37}_{17}Cl$?

   b) In 1000 atoms of chlorine, how many atoms would there be of the isotope

   i) $^{35}_{17}Cl$?

   ii) $^{37}_{17}Cl$?

   c) Use your answer to b) to calculate the relative atomic mass of chlorine (as a weighted average mass).

Concentration

---

1 Calculate the concentration (in mol/dm^3) of the following solutions:

   a) 1.0 mole of sodium hydroxide is dissolved in distilled water to make 500 cm^3 of solution.

   b) 0.2 mole of sodium chloride is dissolved in distilled water to make 1000 cm^3 of solution.

   c) 0.1 mole of sodium nitrate is dissolved in distilled water to make 100 cm^3 of solution.

2 How many moles of silver nitrate would you use to make 100 cm^3 of a 0.1 mol/dm^3 solution?

3 0.1 mole of magnesium chloride ($MgCl_2$) is dissolved in distilled water to make 500 cm^3 of solution.

   a) What is the concentration of the solution, in mol/dm^3, with respect to

   i) magnesium ions?

   ii) chloride ions?

   b) The solution is diluted with distilled water to make 1000 cm^3. What is the new concentration of the magnesium chloride in mol/dm^3?

Gases

1   Copy and complete the table to show the volume (in dm³) you would expect each sample of gas to occupy at both temperatures. (1 dm³ = 1000 cm³)

Sample of gas	Volume (dm³) at 25 °C (298 K) and 1 atmosphere pressure	Volume (dm³) at 0° C (273 K) and 1 atmosphere pressure
1 mole oxygen	24	22.4
2 moles hydrogen		
0.5 mole chlorine		
1.2 moles nitrogen		

2   In a reaction between calcium carbonate and dilute hydrochloric acid, 0.02 dm³ of gas were evolved (as measured at 25 °C and 1 atmosphere).

   a)   What is the name of the gas produced in this reaction?

   b)   Calculate the number of moles of gas produced.

3   The equation for the combustion of methane is shown below.

$$CH_4(g) + 2O_2(g) \longrightarrow CO_2(g) + 2H_2O(g)$$

What volume of oxygen is needed for the complete combustion of 2 dm³ (2000 cm³) methane? Explain your answer.

Energy

1   Halocarbons are compounds containing carbon bonded to elements in group 7 of
    the Periodic Table, the halogens. Some are used as refrigerants, dry cleaning
    solvents and aerosol propellants. An immersion heater was placed into a beaker
    containing a liquid halocarbon of formula $C_2Cl_3F_3$. The temperature of the liquid
    was taken every 30 seconds. The results obtained were as follows:

Time (s)	Temperature (°C)
0	16
30	19
60	23
90	27
120	31
150	35
180	39
210	43
240	47
270	47
300	47
330	47
360 (heating stopped)	47

a) What was the temperature in the laboratory at the start of the experiment?

b) What is the boiling point of the halocarbon?

c) For how long was the halocarbon boiling?

d) A joulemeter in the heating circuit showed that the heater was supplying energy
    at a rate of 2400 joules per minute. How much energy was transferred to the
    halocarbon while it was boiling?

e) During the time the halocarbon was boiling, 37.50 g were vaporised.

   i)   What is the relative molecular mass of the halocarbon?
   ii) How many moles of halocarbon were vaporised?
   iii) Calculate the energy required to vaporise 1 mole of the halocarbon.

f) Why has the use of halocarbons as refrigerants and aerosol propellants been
    considerably reduced?

(Relative atomic masses: C = 12, F = 19, Cl = 35.5)

2 25 cm^3 of ethanol was placed in a boiling tube fitted with a side-arm. An immersion heater was placed in the tube, which was fitted inside a polystyrene jacket as shown in the diagram.

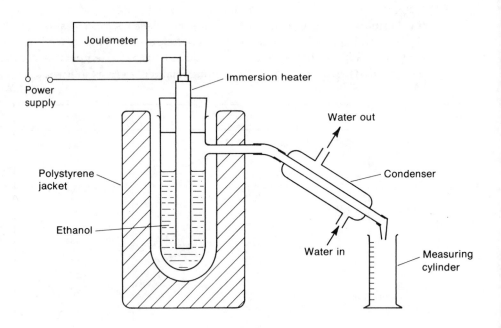

Once the ethanol was boiling at a steady rate, a 10 cm^3 measuring cylinder was placed under the delivery bend to collect ethanol from the condenser. During the time that 5 cm^3 of ethanol was collected, the joulemeter showed that 3.5 kJ of electrical energy was supplied to the heater.

a) Why was the boiling tube placed inside a polystyrene jacket?

b) If the density of ethanol is 0.8 g/cm^3, calculate the mass of 5 cm^3 of ethanol. (Formula: mass = volume × density)

c) The mass of one mole of ethanol is 46 g. Calculate the heat of vaporisation of ethanol in kJ/mol.

d) i)   Why was collection of ethanol *not* begun as soon as some ethanol began to· flow out of the condenser?

    ii) Write down two sources of error in this experiment, and state how the method could be modified to reduce them.

e) Would you expect the value for the heat of vaporisation of ethanol obtained from this experiment to be greater or less (numerically) than the true value? Explain your choice.

3 This question is about an experiment to determine the heat of combustion of methanol. A sample of methanol was placed in a wick burner and weighed. The burner was then transferred to the apparatus shown below.

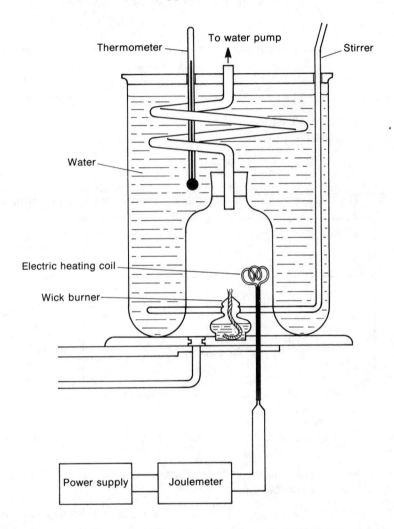

The burner was lit, and the water allowed to rise through 10.0 °C before the burner was extinguished. When the apparatus had returned to room temperature, an electric heating coil was used to heat the water in the apparatus, and a joulemeter used to find the energy input needed to cause a 10.0 °C temperature rise.

The results of the experiment are given below:

Mass of burner and methanol at the start	118.50 g
Mass of burner and methanol at the end	116.65 g
Energy required to give 10.0 °C rise in temperature	42 100 J

a) Calculate the mass of methanol burnt during the experiment.

b) Explain why it was necessary to stir the water continuously during heating.

c) What was the purpose of the water pump?

d) i) How does this method compensate for heat loss from the apparatus?

   ii) Name one other source of error in the experiment.

e) Use the formula

$$\text{heat of combustion of methanol} = \frac{32}{\text{mass of methanol burnt (g)}} \times \frac{\text{energy released (J)}}{1000}$$

to calculate the heat of combustion of methanol in kJ/mol.

f) Write a balanced chemical equation for the complete combustion of methanol (CH_4O).

4 The table shows some information about some hydrocarbons known as **alkanes**.

Name	Molecular formula	Relative molecular mass	Boiling point (°C)	Heat of combustion (kJ/mol)
Methane	CH_4	16	−161	−890
Ethane		30	−89	−1560
Propane	C_3H_8	44	−42	−2220
Butane	C_4H_{10}	58		−2877
Pentane	C_5H_{12}	72	+36	−3509
Hexane	C_6H_{14}	86	+69	

a) Use the pattern in the formulae to predict the formula of ethane.

b) i) How do the boiling points change as the relative molecular mass of the hydrocarbons increases?

   ii) Use a graphical method to estimate the boiling point of butane.

c) Calculate the difference between successive values of the heats of combustion, and use your result to estimate the heat of combustion of hexane in kJ/mol.

d) Which of the following hydrocarbons belong to the alkane family?

$$C_{10}H_{22} \quad\quad C_6H_6 \quad\quad C_{12}H_{26} \quad\quad C_2H_4 \quad\quad C_{25}H_{52}$$

Electrochemistry

In answering the following questions, you may need to use this information:

number of coulombs (C) = current passed (A) × time (s)

The charge on 1 mole of electrons (6×10^{23} electrons) is 96 500 C.

1 a) Calculate the charge passed during electrolysis of a solution of silver nitrate, if a current of 0.1 A flowed for 2 hours 41 minutes.

b) How many moles of silver metal would be deposited at the cathode?

c) What additional information would you need to calculate the mass of silver deposited?

Show your working in all parts of this question.

2 What current would be needed to deposit 0.5 mole of nickel from a nickel(II) sulphate solution in 2 hours? Explain how you obtained your answer.

3 A current of 0.5 A flowing for 3 hours 40 minutes deposits 0.068 mole of silver from an aqueous solution of silver nitrate (containing the ions Ag^+ and NO_3^-). Use this data to calculate the charge in coulombs on one electron.

4 An experiment was set up to measure the heat of reaction, ΔH, for the reaction

$$Zn(s) + Cu^{2+}(aq) \longrightarrow Zn^{2+}(aq) + Cu(s)$$

25 cm^3 of 0.2 M copper(II) sulphate solution were transferred to a suitable container and the temperature of the solution was recorded. 0.5 g of zinc filings was then added and mixed continuously with the solution.

The highest temperature reached by the mixture was recorded.

At the end of the experiment, it was noticed that the blue colour of the copper(II) sulphate solution had completely disappeared.

Results
Initial temperature of solution = 18 °C
Highest temperature reached   = 28 °C

Data
Relative atomic mass of Zn = 65

a) How many moles of zinc atoms are added in the experiment?

b) How many moles of Cu^{2+} ions are there in 25 cm^3 of 0.2 M copper(II) sulphate solution?

c) What would the effect of repeating this experiment using 0.5 g of zinc metal sheet instead of 0.5 g of zinc filings?

d) How many kJ of heat are liberated when the 0.5 g of zinc is added to the 25 cm^3 of 0.2 M copper(II) sulphate solution?

5 The diagram shows an experiment to electroplate a nickel spoon with silver.

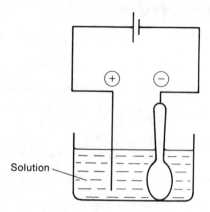

Solution

a) Suggest a suitable material for the anode.

b) Name a compound that could be dissolved to make the solution.

c) Explain fully what happens
   i)   at the cathode
   ii) at the anode
   iii) in the electrolyte.

d) For the electrolyte you have named in part b), write ionic equations for the reactions at the
   i)   cathode
   ii) anode.

e) During the electroplating experiment, a current of 0.2 A is passed for 5 hours. What mass of silver would be deposited on the spoon? (Relative atomic mass of silver = 107.)

6   The diagram below shows the simultaneous electrolysis of a molten salt and a solution of another salt in water.

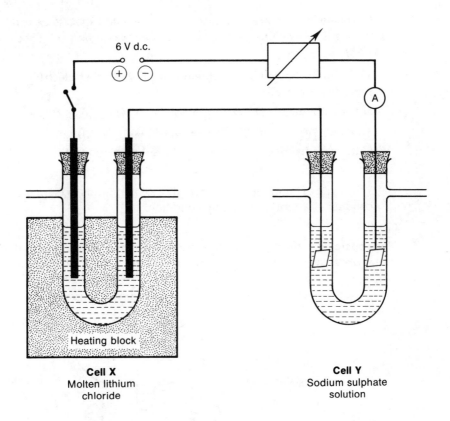

Cell X
Molten lithium
chloride

Cell Y
Sodium sulphate
solution

Cell X contains lithium chloride that is kept molten by means of an electrical heating block. The cathode is a steel rod and the anode is a carbon rod.

Cell X is connected in series with cell Y, which contains water in which a few grams of sodium sulphate have been dissolved. The electrodes of cell Y are platinum foil.

Any gases produced at the electrodes can be collected by connecting the side-arms of the tubes to gas syringes.

A current, kept constant at 2.0 A, was passed through the cells for 80 minutes. This resulted in 0.7 g of lithium being deposited at the cathode of cell X.

(Lithium metal melts at 180 °C and has a density of 0.5 g/cm^3. Lithium chloride melts at 613 °C and has a density of 2.07 g/cm^3.)

a)   Show on a copy of the diagram, by shading and a label, where you would expect the lithium metal to collect.

b)   Calculate the number of moles of electrons (faradays) used to produce 0.7 g of lithium.

c)   The lithium ion is Li$^+$. Calculate the mass of 1 mole of lithium atoms. (Show your working.)

d) No electrolysis took place until the lithium chloride was molten. Explain what change took place at the melting point of lithium chloride to account for this.

e) Calculate the volume of chlorine gas you would expect to be produced in cell X during the same time that 0.7 g of lithium was produced. (The chloride ion is Cl^-.)

f) The solution in cell Y was initially at pH 7. During electrolysis the following reactions occurred:

at the cathode $4H_3O^+(aq) + 4e^- \longrightarrow 4H_2O(l) + 2H_2(g)$

at the anode $6H_2O(l) \longrightarrow 4H_3O^+(aq) + O_2(g) + 4e^-$

State what happens to the pH of the solution round the cathode and explain why.

g) What type of bonding is present in those compounds or elements that will never conduct electricity under any conditions?

7 The apparatus in the diagram below was used to investigate electrical cells. Different metal plates were put into the solution and the voltage was measured.

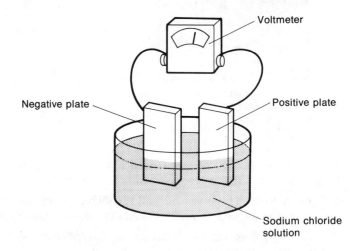

a) Explain how a voltage is produced.

The results in the table below were obtained when different metals were used as the positive and negative plates.

Positive plate	Negative plate	Voltmeter reading (V)
Copper	Tin	0.5
Tin	Zinc	0.6
Zinc	Magnesium	1.7

Copper and zinc plates were then put into the solution.

b) Explain why zinc was the negative plate.

c) What would the voltmeter reading be?

d) With copper as the positive plate and zinc as the negative plate, write ionic equations for the reactions

    i)   at the negative plate

    ii) at the positive plate.

e) What prediction can you make concerning the voltage obtained by using one copper and one zinc plate?

8 Some twenty years ago, the first electrical cells to use the metal lithium were developed. They are now widely used in devices such as watches, cameras and electronic instruments. The diagram below shows the construction of a typical lithium–manganese dioxide coin cell.

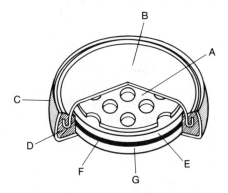

Key
A. Current collector. Sheet of perforated stainless steel.
B. Stainless steel top cap. Functions as negative terminal of cell.
C. Stainless steel cell can. Functions as positive terminal of cell.
D. Polypropylene closure. Highly impermeable to water vapour and prevents moisture entering the cell after it has been sealed.
E. Lithium negative electrode. Punched from sheet lithium.
F. Separator containing electrolyte, a non-aqueous solution of lithium perchlorate in a mixture of propylene carbonate and dimethoxyethane.
G. Manganese dioxide positive electrode. The cathode is made from a highly active electrolytic oxide.

a) State *two* advantages of lithium as a material for use in electrical cells.

b) Explain the main problem when using lithium in electrical cells.

c) What *two* features of the cell shown above are designed to overcome the problem described in b)?

The diagram below shows part of the discharge reaction in the lithium–manganese dioxide cell.

Lithium anode	Electrolyte $LiClO_4$ (non-aqueous)	Manganese dioxide cathode	Cathode current collector (stainless steel)

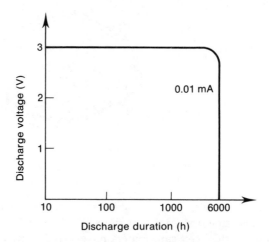

d) Write a balanced equation for the reaction taking place at the anode (A).

e) Label the diagram at B, C and D to indicate the nature of the particles that are moving, and the direction of their movement.

The graph below shows the discharge curve of a typical lithium–manganese dioxide coin cell discharged at a rate of 0.01 mA.

f) Calculate the amount of energy stored in the cell. (Assume 100% of the energy is given out during discharge and ignore the rounded shoulder of the graph. The time scale is linear between the numbered points.) Show your working clearly.

g) Sketch the discharge curve you would expect from a discharge rate of 0.1 mA. (Assume the scale on the time axis is linear between the numbered points.)

h) How many moles of electrons are released during discharge? Give your answer to *two* significant figures.

i) The relative atomic mass of lithium is 6.9. How many grams of lithium are used in the cell? (Assume all of it is used up during discharge.)

6 ATOMS AND RADIOACTIVITY

Isotopes

1 a) What are **isotopes** of an element?

b) The diagram below shows an atom of the most common isotope of oxygen, $^{16}_{8}O$.

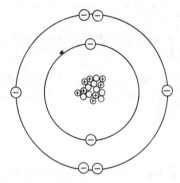

Two other isotopes of oxygen exist, $^{17}_{8}O$ and $^{18}_{8}O$. Draw similar diagrams to show the atomic structure of these two isotopes

c) Copy and complete the passage below choosing the words from this list to fill in the blanks (each word may be used more than once):

    unstable   **radioactive**   **rays**   **particles**   **nucleus**   **isotope**

All elements can have more than one _____. Many of them are _____. The _____ undergoes a change. When this happens α _____, β _____ or γ _____ may be emitted from the _____. This is called _____ decay.

2 a) Explain what is meant by the **half-life** of a radioactive isotope.

b) A sample of iodine-128 was monitored in an experiment and the following results obtained:

Time elapsed (minutes)	Count rate (counts/minute)
17	7080
29	5192
50	2816
60	2198
76	1364
105	662

The background count in the laboratory during the experiment was 80 counts/minute.

  i)   Explain what the 'background count' is, and list two contributions to it.
  ii) Plot a graph of corrected count against time and use it to find the half-life of iodine-128.

3 The isotope $^{14}_{6}C$ has a half-life of 5600 years.

a) How many

  i)   protons
  ii) neutrons are there in a nucleus of carbon-14?

b) After how long would a sample of carbon-14 decay to $\frac{1}{32}$ of the original count-rate?

c) Suggest why carbon-14 has been particularly useful in biochemical research.

d) Describe experiments using carbon-14 which show that

  i)   the carbon dioxide breathed out by a small mammal comes from glucose eaten.
  ii) carbon dioxide is absorbed by a leaf during photosynthesis.
  iii) sugars made in leaves during photosynthesis are transported to other parts of the plant in the phloem.

Decay Processes

1 a) Radon has a half-life of four days. How long will it take for $\frac{7}{8}$ of a sample of radon to decay?

   b) Radium has a half-life of 1622 years. How long will it take for a 1.6 g sample of radium to decay until only 0.1 g remains?

2 A small domestic fire alarm contains a sample of radioactive americium placed close to two charged plates. Smoke particles from a fire cause a drop in the small current flowing between the plates, triggering the alarm.

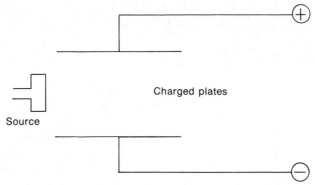

   a) What effect, due to the americium, causes a small current to flow between the plates?

   b) Explain how the presence of smoke particles causes the drop in current which triggers the alarm.

   c) The operating instructions state that the unit should be wiped and vacuum cleaned carefully at least every six months. Suggest a reason for this.

3 Plastic sheet can be made by an extrusion process known as calendering. The thickness of the sheet, which must not vary too much, can be monitored using a radioactive source and detector as shown in the diagram:

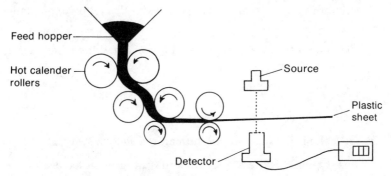

a) Which type of source, alpha, beta or gamma, would *not* be suitable for this application? Explain your choice.

b) What is the name of the type of detector commonly used to detect radioactivity?

c) Explain how the source and detector can be used to monitor the thickness of the sheet.

4 Some forms of cancer can be treated using radiotherapy. Before treatment, the position of a tumour in the body is found. Two beams of radiation can then be directed at the tumour, each of just over one-half of the intensity needed to destroy tissue.

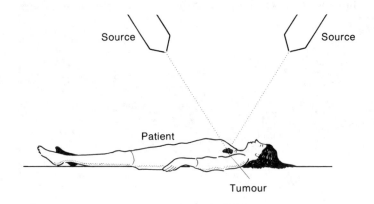

a) Explain why this procedure is of greater benefit to the patient than using a single (more powerful) beam.

b) Explain how rotating a single powerful source (or the patient) about an axis through the tumour is an equally useful method.

c) Why are the radioactive isotopes used in *diagnosis* almost always gamma sources?

5 Describe the use of radioactive isotopes in the following situations. In each case say

i) whether a suitable isotope should have a half-life measured in seconds, hours, days or years

ii) whether the type of source (α, β or γ) is important.

a) tracing leaks in underground pipes

b) revealing blockages in the human circulatory system

c) testing the thickness of cardboard during manufacture

6 a) Write down the following particle symbols and give the common name for each.

   i) ^1_1H

   ii) $^{0}_{-1}\beta$

   iii) ^2_1H

   iv) ^1_0N

   v) ^4_2He

b) Draw diagrams which show the structure of particles iii) and v).

7 Copy and complete the following nuclear reactions.

a) $^{24}_{12}Mg + ^1_0n \longrightarrow ^{24}_{11}Na + \boxed{}$

b) $^{24}_{11}Na \longrightarrow \boxed{} Mg + ^{0}_{-1}\beta$

c) $^3_1H \longrightarrow ^3_2He + \boxed{}$

d) $^{236}_{92}U \longrightarrow ^{144}_{56}Ba + ^1_0n + \boxed{} Kr$

e) $^7_3Li + ^1_1H \longrightarrow ^4_2He + \boxed{}$

Theme 3

Earth Science

1 GEOLOGY

Water

1   Look carefully at the diagram below which shows part of the **water cycle** in nature, and answer the questions which follow.

a)   What is happening at A and B on the diagram?

b)   Where is the purest water to be found?

c)   Explain how smoke from the factory (G) could affect life in the lake (F).

d)   i)   If the farmer puts too much fertiliser on his fields at area C, what will happen to the excess?

    ii)   How will this affect the plant life in the sea?

e)   How could the cutting down of large areas of forest such as E affect the water cycle?

f)   Explain how this deforestation could also lead to

    i)   soil erosion
    ii)   flooding
    iii) silting up of the river

g)   Explain how it is possible that one of the residents at D has used some of the water which the farmer drank a year ago.

2 Look at the drawing of the **water cycle**, and use it to answer the following questions.

a) What is causing the seawater to evaporate?

b) Say what *two* processes, apart from evaporation from the sea, might be adding water to the air.

c) What causes the water vapour to condense as it rises?

d) Choose one of the explanations A–D to complete the sentence about rainwater.

   Rainwater is not salty because _____

   A. most rain comes from freshwater lakes.
   B. the salt is left behind when the water evaporates.
   C. the salt is left behind when water condenses.
   D. the salt is broken down by sunlight.

3 a) Why does the amount of hardness in water differ from place to place?

b) What would you notice if a small amount of soap (sodium stearate) is shaken with this hard water?

c) Why should this hard water **not** be used in a hot water system?

d) Explain the difference between temporary and permanent hardness, giving *one* cause of each.

e) Describe *one* method of removing
   i)   temporary hardness
   ii) permanent hardness

4 An ion-exchange column removes hardness from water. The following diagram shows what happens as the water passes through the ion-exchange column.

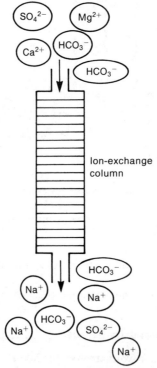

a) No soap is used in a dishwasher. Why, therefore, is it necessary to remove hardness from the water used by the dishwasher?

b) Write a balanced equation, with state symbols, to explain your answer to a).

c) Explain the changes that take place in the ion-exchange column.

d) After a time, the ion-exchange column will no longer remove hardness from the water. Explain why.

e) Suggest how the ion-exchange column can be recharged so it is able to remove hardness from the water again.

f) Dishwashers have a salt compartment that needs to be kept filled. If the salt is used up, the glassware looks 'cloudy' after washing.

Explain the action of the salt in a dishwasher and describe what happens if it is absent.

Rocks, Soils and Minerals

1 What can be learnt from a study of

a) rock texture?

b) rock colour(s)?

2 Two students were asked to compare the ability of two samples of limestone to absorb water. The methods they chose are outlined in the table.

Emma	*Steven*
1. Take 1 cm³ cube of each type of lime-stone.	1. Take two 10.0 g samples of each type of limestone.
2. Put 50.0 cm³ water in each of two measuring cylinders.	2. Place each sample in a beaker containing 50.0 cm³ water.
3. Put one sample of limestone in each measuring cylinder.	3. After 20 minutes, remove each sample and re-weigh.
4. Note the new volume reading on the measuring cylinders after 5 minutes.	4. Calculate the gain in mass of each sample.

a) For each method state

i) one source of inaccuracy

ii) how the accuracy of the result could be improved

b) How would Emma use her results to decide which sample was more absorbent?

c) Jane noticed that one of Steven's samples had broken into two fragments. Would this affect the result of the experiment? Explain your answer.

Two samples of another sedimentary rock, sandstone, are shown below. Which would you expect to be more absorbent and why?

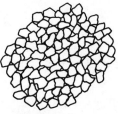
Specimen A

Specimen B

3 Pair these groups of words to form sentences about soil:

a) **Soil is formed from rock**   in colour than subsoil.

b) **Weathering agents include**   remains of dead organisms, called
                                                    humus.

c) **Topsoil is generally darker**   important for plant growth.

d) **Topsoil contains decaying**   rain, wind, snow and frost.

e) **If a sample of soil is shaken in water**   gravel, humus, mineral salts, water
   and allowed to stand   and air.

f) **The finest particles of soil are**   by the action of weathering agents.

g) **Soil contains sand, clay,**   nitrogen, phosphorus, potassium
                                                    and magnesium.

h) **Mineral salts in soil water are**   filled with air and water.

i) **The kind and amount of minerals in**   the type of rock the soil was formed
   soil depend on   from and the activities of bacteria.

j) **Some important elements in mineral**   clay particles with a diameter less
   salts are   than 0.002 mm.

k) **Spaces between the soil particles are**   the larger particles settle first.

4 Explain the importance of the following components of the soil:

a) humus   b) lime   c) mineral salts   d) soil water   e) soil air

5 A sample of soil was placed in a tall glass measuring cylinder with a large volume of
water. It was then shaken and left to settle completely. The results are shown in this
diagram:

a) Copy the diagram and replace the
   letters A–F with correct labels.

b) Which soil particles settle first and why?

c) Why does part B appear cloudy?

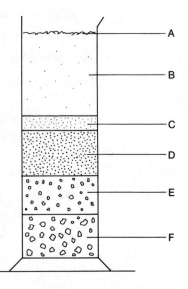

6 Below are seven pairs of statements about soil. Construct a table with two headings like the one below. For each pair of descriptions, decide which one applies to sandy soil and which one to clay soil; then complete the table.

Sandy soil	Clay soil

a) Composed mainly of large particles
   Composed mainly of fine particles

b) Contains large air spaces
   Contains small air spaces

c) Poorly drained and aerated
   Well drained and aerated

d) Useful chemicals are washed out when it rains
   Holds on to useful chemicals well

e) Rich in plant food
   Poor in plant food

f) Loose, light and easy to dig
   Cold, heavy and difficult to dig

7 An analysis of two soil samples carried out by a gardener gave the following results:

	Sample A	Sample B
Sand	85%	22%
Clay	14%	70%
Humus	1%	8%

a) Give *one* advantage and *one* disadvantage of each soil sample for growing young plants.

b) How could you improve soil from sample A so that plants would grow better in it?

c) How could you improve soil of type B?

d) The ideal garden soil is called **loam**.
   i) What, roughly, should its composition be?
   ii) Why is loam better for plant growth than sandy or clay soil?

e) i) Why is peaty soil not very fertile?
   ii) Why is it improved by adding lime?

f) Why is chalky soil alkaline?

8 a) Earthworms live in the soil. Describe *four* ways in which the earthworm is useful to gardeners.

b) Name *two* soil organisms which are pests and say why they are pests.

9   The diagram below shows a landscape that is being altered by water, wind, ice, temperature change and by plant roots. Look at the diagram and answer the questions which follow.

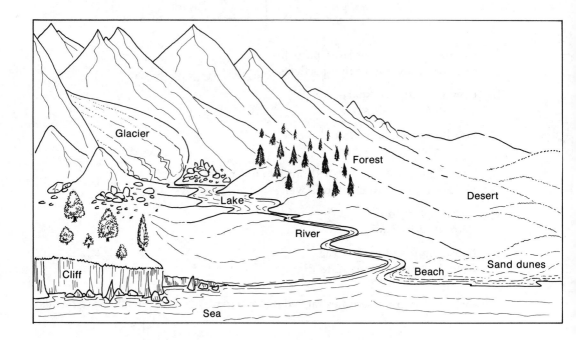

a)   Describe *two* ways in which the cliff could be broken down.

b)   i) What is a glacier?

ii) Suggest *two* ways that the movement of ice down the glacier would affect the rock that it is in contact with.

iii) Why are rock particles deposited at the foot of the glacier?

c)   Pick out *one* other place where rock is being broken down and explain how this happens.

d)   How are rock particles carried to the sea?

e)   What sort of rock will eventually be formed as layer after layer of rock particles are deposited on the bed of the lake?

f)   The mountains are found to be made of a very hard igneous rock which has large crystals in it. Describe how this rock would have been formed.

10 a) Explain how each of the following can produce soil erosion:
   i) deforestation
   ii) overgrazing
   iii) bad agricultural practices

b) Suggest ways of reducing soil erosion.

11

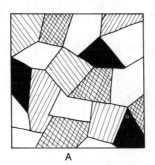

A

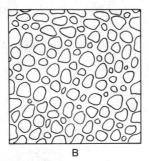

B

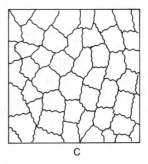

C

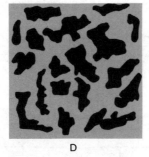

D

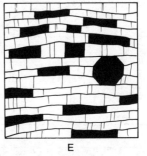

E

Use the key provided to identify the rock specimens A–E above.

1. Does the rock show a 'mosaic' pattern of crystals, or *appear* to have fragments of one material embedded in another?	Crystal mosaic – go to 4 Fragments – go to 2
2. Are the fragments aligned?	Yes – SCHIST No – go to 3
3. Does the rock appear coarse or fine-grained?	Coarse – GABBRO Fine – ORTHOQUARTZITE
4. Are there crystals of more than one mineral?	Yes – GRANITE No – METAQUARTZITE

12   The diagram shows the rock structure under part of England.

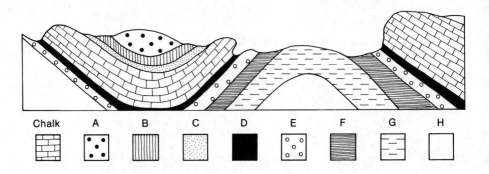

Write down the letters of the rocks shown in the key which are *younger* than chalk.
Explain your answer.

13

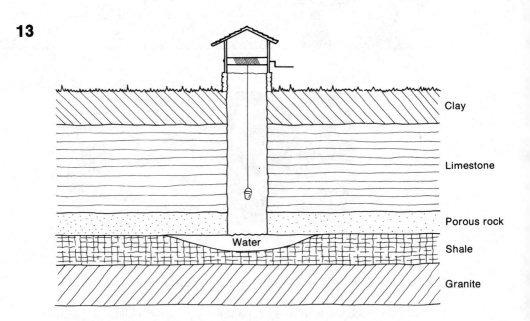

The diagram above shows the layers of rock beneath a well.

a)   Give *one* origin of the underground water.

b)   Name *one* sedimentary and *one* igneous rock shown in the diagram.

c)   i) What is meant by 'hard water'?
      ii) Would you expect water drawn from this well to be hard or soft? Explain
          your answer.

d)   Describe *one* problem caused by hard water in the home.

14 Under the Earth's crust there is hot, molten rock. In some places water drains down to the hot rocks above the molten material and is sent back up again as a geyser or as a hot spring. The energy from these springs is used in some countries such as Iceland. The diagram below shows the typical geological structure of an area where hot springs might occur.

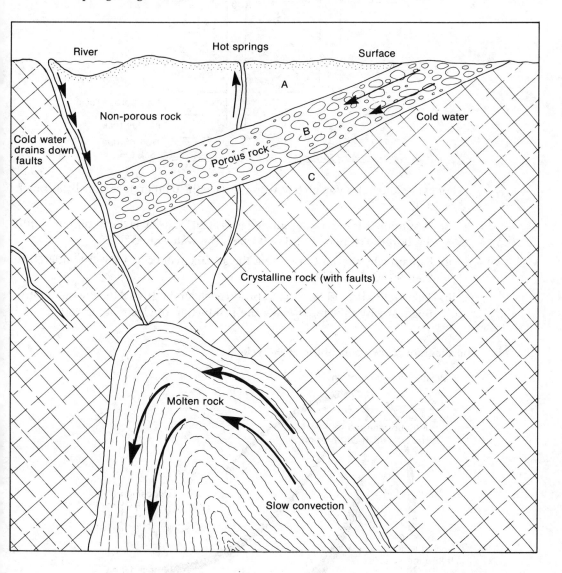

a) i) Which one of the rocks labelled A, B and C is most likely to be igneous? Give *one* reason for your choice.

   ii) Suggest *one* cause of the fault lines shown in the diagram.

b) Britain does not have any natural geysers but artificial geysers have been made. Two bore-holes are drilled down into the rocks. Cold water enters by one hole and returns to the surface at a higher temperature (see next page).

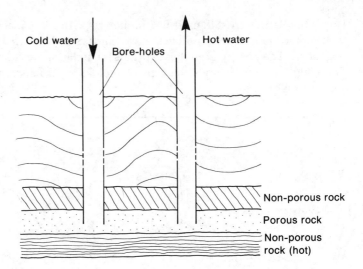

For every kilometre you go below the surface the temperature rises by as much as 40 °C.

i) Assuming that the water pumped in is at 10 °C, what is the minimum depth the bore-holes need to go to, to heat the water to 90 °C?

ii) Explain why the water reaching the surface will be at a lower temperature than 90 °C.

iii) This method could be used to produce steam to drive a turbine-generator. Suggest why this might make the production of electricity cheaper.

15 The diagram shows part of the **rock cycle**.

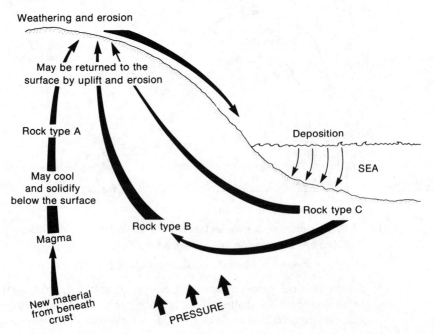

a) What names are given to the three types of rock, A, B and C, shown in the diagram?

b) Suggest *two* features you would expect sedimentary rocks to have.

c) Suggest *two* conditions necessary to convert sedimentary rocks to metamorphic rocks.

d) Suggest *two* methods by which rocks at the surface might be weathered.

16

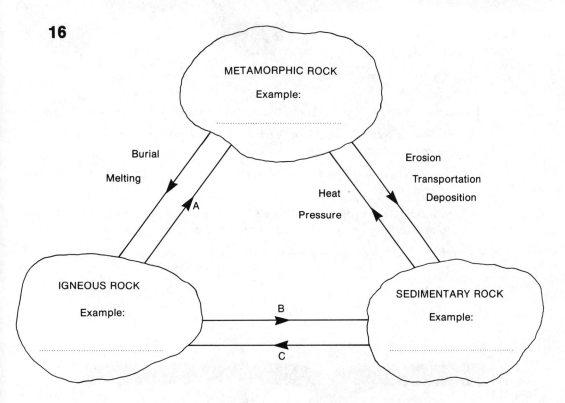

The above diagram shows processes occurring in the rock cycle, which inter-convert the three types of rock.

a) Copy the diagram and add the processes which are missing at A, B and C.

b) Add the name of one example of each type of rock.

c) Explain what the words **erosion, transportation** and **deposition** mean as applied to the rock cycle.

d) Why are sedimentary rocks more likely to be metamorphosed than igneous rocks?

e) Name the two major driving forces for change within the rock cycle.

17

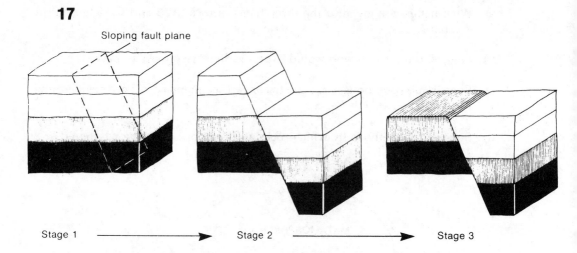

Sloping fault plane

Stage 1 ——————————→ Stage 2 ——————————→ Stage 3

The diagrams show three stages in the evolution of the land near a fault zone.

a) In stage 1, were the rocks on each side of the fault under compression or tension? Explain your answer.

b) Describe the changes which have occurred between stages 2 and 3, and give two possible causes.

c) Draw a diagram, equivalent to stage 3, showing one possible outcome when the forces acting on the rocks are in the opposite direction to those in this example.

d) What is the origin of the forces which caused the movement?

18

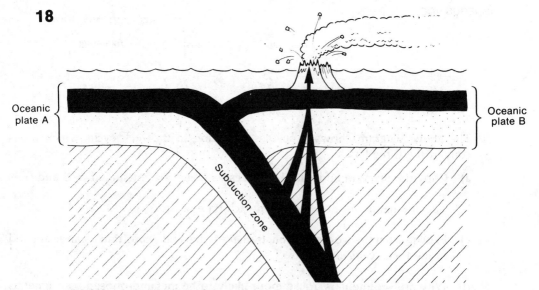

Oceanic plate A

Oceanic plate B

Subduction zone

Mobile plates in the Earth's crust collide as a result of tectonic action. At destructive plate margins, crust is forced downwards in a subduction zone. In the example shown, two oceanic plates are involved.

a) In which direction is each of the plates moving?

b) Give *two* reasons why rock forced downwards into a subduction zone is likely to melt, leading to volcanism.

c) What would be found above a subduction zone where two continental plates are colliding?

d) What is believed to be the driving force for tectonic action?

19 The article reproduced below appeared in *The Daily Telegraph* of 26th September, 1984. Read the article carefully and answer the questions which follow.

VOLCANO ASH DIMS SUNLIGHT

By IAN WARD in Manila

A SIX MILE-HIGH dense cloud of ash hung yesterday over the entire southern Luzon province of Albay, where the Mayon volcano continues its spectacular display.

Thousands fled villages threatened by flows of lava and mud.

The aerial blanket of ash transformed the noon sky over the province into a murky half-light as farmers around the volcano abandoned vast stretches of rice fields now lying under large layers of mud.

Philippine Airlines removed all jets from its southern Luzon schedules, replacing them with propeller-driven aircraft as a safety precaution against airborne volcanic ash, which can quickly snuff out jet engines.

Boulders big as cars

The Philippine Civil Aviation Authority continued to warn foreign commercial aircraft to fly clear of the ash clouds, which were drifting in several directions from the erupting crater, but have been meticulously plotted by satellite technology.

Throughout the day Mayon hurled boulders as big as cars into the air and down its slopes. To add to the awesome display flashes of lightning repeatedly hit the top of the belching cone of the volcano.

But vulcanologists said seismic readings were now suggesting that the worst of the eruption, which began with a huge blast on September 9, was over.

Many evacuees have been treated for burns and lung problems associated with inhalation of gases and ash, but no deaths have been reported as a result of the volcano's present eruption.

a) Why did the population flee from their valleys?

b) Why were jets forbidden from flying near the volcanic eruption?

c) The eruption produced liquid, solid and gaseous materials.

  i) Name *one* solid and *one* liquid which were thrown out.

  ii) Name *one* gas which escapes from a volcano.

20 The map below shows part of the world with plate boundaries and plate movement indicated.

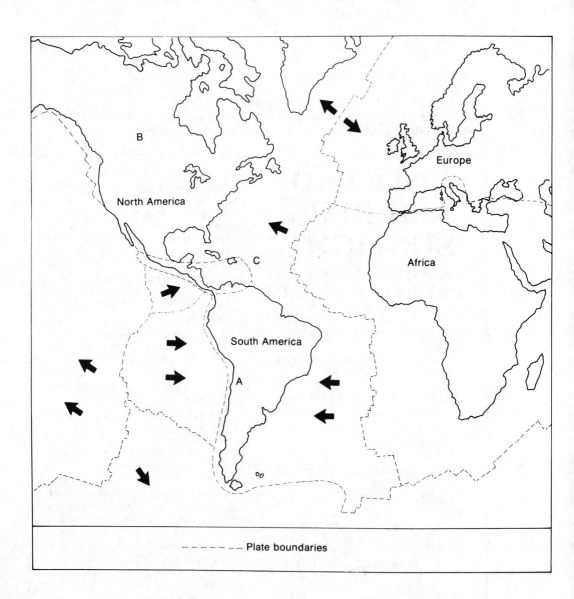

a) Trace the map and add labels to indicate one constructive and one destructive plate margin.

b) At which of the sites A, B or C would you expect to find
   i) volcanism?
   ii) mountain building?

21

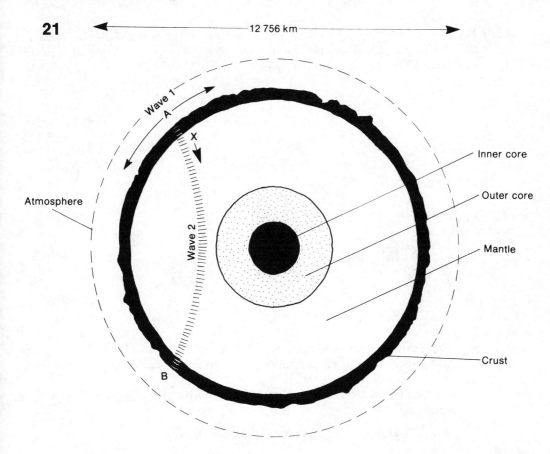

The diagram (not to scale) shows the layered internal structure of the Earth. An earthquake occurring at X, directly below the epicentre (A), is detected at location B. Shock waves arrive at B over a period of 15 minutes.

a)   What name is given to point X?

b)   Which wave is a P wave?

c)   An earthquake occurs when forces inside the Earth cause large masses of rock to fracture and move. Waves from the Earthquake travel through the Earth and along the crust.

   i) Explain why the wave travelling through the Earth takes a curved path.

   ii) Give two reasons why waves travelling along the crust take longer to reach location B than those travelling through the mantle.

   iii) Would you expect earthquakes to originate below a depth of 1000 km? Explain your answer.

d)   Suggest one result of a major earthquake occurring beneath the sea.

e)   Give two pieces of information which suggest that the Earth has a core containing iron.

22   The map shows the location of two regions of granite in Scotland. It is believed that they were once part of a single granite mass. Movement of rock masses along a fault line slowly separated the two samples.

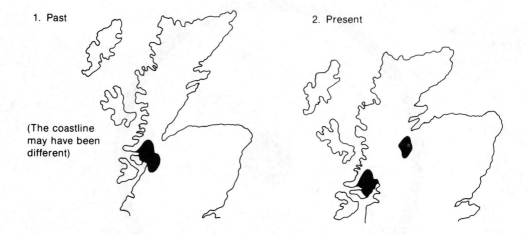

1. Past

2. Present

(The coastline may have been different)

a)   Trace map number 2 and draw on it the fault line responsible for the separation. Add arrows to indicate the direction of movement on each side of the fault.

b)   Choose a timescale from those listed below in which this change is likely to have occurred.

         5 years   5000 years   5 million years

c)   The distance between the granite locations today is approximately 100 km. Using your answer to part b), calculate the average rate of displacement in centimetres per year.

d)   What causes displacements such as this?

23   Some chemical elements decay with age, producing radioactivity in the process. Potassium turns into argon, and rubidium into strontium. Uranium-238 is an element which decays through a series of radioactive products to finish as lead-206. In any uranium ore the proportion of lead-206 increases with time. The decay occurs at a constant rate, the half-life of uranium-238 being 4 500 000 000 years.

Explain briefly how scientists can use this information to determine the age of rocks.

2 ATMOSPHERE

Air

1 a) The inside of a boiling tube was coated with vaseline. Iron filings were added to the tube, which was shaken. The filings were then poured out, leaving a layer of finely divided iron stuck to the inside wall of the boiling tube, which was placed upside-down in a water trough as shown below.

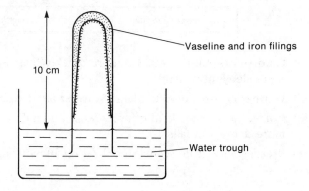

After several days, the level of water had risen 2 cm up the boiling tube, of which 10 cm in total was above the water level in the trough.

b) i) Explain why the water level rose in the tube.
    ii) What approximate value does this experiment give for the percentage by volume of oxygen in air? Show how you arrived at your answer.

The following gases are found in dry air:

       helium   **carbon dioxide**   **nitrogen**   **oxygen**

Which of the gases in the list are

c) a monatomic element?

d) a diatomic element?

e) a compound?

f) Which gas is the least chemically reactive?

2

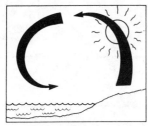

Day: on-shore breeze　　　　　　　Night: off-shore breeze

The diagrams show the direction of coastal breezes by day and night.

a)　Copy the diagrams.

b)　Below are some statements about coastal breezes. Make a copy of the table below. Consider each pair of statements and decide which one goes into which column in the following table, then write in the statements.

During the day	During the night

i)　Land (rocks, soil) warms up more quickly than water/Water cools down more slowly than land.

ii)　Warmer air rises over the land/Warmer air rises over the sea.

iii)　Colder air over the land is more dense and falls/Colder air over the sea is more dense and falls.

iv)　Breezes blow from sea to land/Breezes blow from land to sea.

3　Read the passage below. Use the information in the passage and your knowledge to answer the questions which follow.

> Over lengthy periods climate can change. A long-term shift of only 1 °C is enough to trigger such profound changes as the Little Ice Age in Western Europe, which peaked in the late 17th century. A drop of 4 °C is enough to bring on a full ice age. At the moment we are in one of the warmest phases of the past 1000 years. (In the northern hemisphere between 1881 and 1983, the warmest year was 1981.)
>
> Climatic change is the norm. The one thing that we can be sure about with regard to future climate is that it will feature deep-seated shifts, even if we leave it to get on with its own natural course – without disrupting it by, for example, contributing to carbon dioxide build-up in the atmosphere. This has major implications for our capacity to keep producing food. Throughout the world, climate is a critical factor in agriculture. During the late 1960s, the drought in the Sahel brought disaster to entire nations. In 1972 another drought inflicted such damage on the Soviet wheat crop that it helped to quadruple world prices within two years. In 1974, a delayed monsoon in India wrought havoc for millions of people. In 1975 pulses of cold air ravaged Brazil's coffee crop, causing inflationary upheavals in coffee prices around the world.
>
> Conversely, of course, a stable climate, or rather a climate with slow and predictable change, can be a tremendous asset that can basically enrich our lives.
>
> *Adapted from* Gaia Atlas of Planet Management.

a) Explain why 'climate is a critical factor in agriculture'.

b)   i) How are we 'contributing to carbon dioxide build-up in the atmosphere'?

ii) What effect is this build-up likely to have on the Earth's climate?

c)   i) What happened to coffee prices in 1976?

ii) Explain why this happened.

d) In recent years there have been droughts in Ethiopia and the Sudan. What was the effect on the people living in these areas?

e) What is meant by a 'stable climate'?

f) Why do you think the author describes a stable climate as 'a tremendous asset'?

4

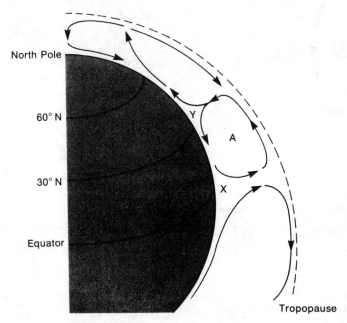

The diagram shows the movement of air between the Earth's surface and the tropopause in the northern hemisphere during April. Air rising above the equator can move in a northerly or southerly direction, returning to ground level about one-third of the way to the poles. Cold polar air descends and moves underneath warmer air from the equator. These general patterns persist throughout the year.

a) Describe how the height of the tropopause varies in the hemisphere.

b) What name is given to the transfer of heat by circulating currents like those around point A in the diagram?

c) What causes air to rise above point X on the equator?

d) Would you expect the air pressure at sea level near point X to be greater or less than that near point Y? Explain your answer.

e) The wind patterns shown in the diagram, drift north or south on a seasonal basis. Suggest an explanation for this drift.

Pollution

1

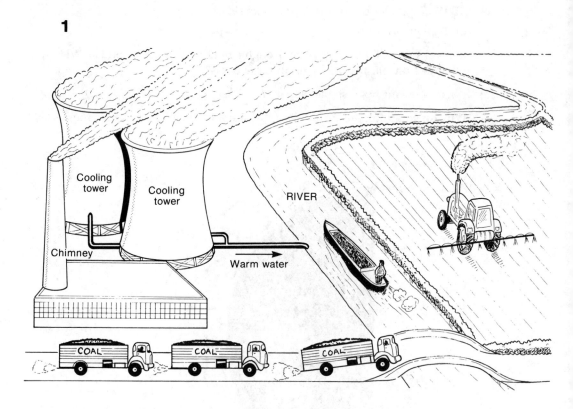

Look at the diagram and list all the examples of pollution you can see. Record your answer as shown below:

Name of pollutant	Where produced	One effect of this pollutant

2 In an attempt to get rid of a type of mosquito which was infesting a lake, the authorities sprayed the lake with the insecticide DDT. This appeared to be successful, since the mosquitoes died while other animals and plants seemed to be little affected. Consequently the treatment was repeated the next year. Some years later many large fish-eating birds were found to be dead or dying. When their bodies were analysed they were found to contain large amounts of DDT. Other animals and plants were examined and the results are shown in the table.

Organisms	Amount of DDT per unit mass
Small fish	10 units
Animal plankton	5 units
Plant plankton	1 unit
Large fish	100 units
Lake water	0.3 units
Grebes (fish-eating birds)	1600 units

a) Draw a food chain for the lake.

b) Why was such a high dosage of DDT found in grebes?

c) Why is DDT known as a persistent pesticide?

d) What steps can be taken to reduce pollution by pesticides?

3 Nitrogen is the most common gas in our atmosphere. Normally it is inert, but at high temperatures it can react with oxygen. A gas formed in this reaction, nitrogen monoxide, may lead to acid rain. Although nitrogen monoxide is neutral, it reacts instantly on contact with air to give the acidic gas nitrogen dioxide.

a) What does 'inert' mean?

b) Explain how nitrogen dioxide is produced by each of the following sources:

    i) a coal-fired power station

    ii) a motor car

c) To reduce the pollution caused by nitrogen oxides, motor cars which run on unleaded petrol can be fitted with a catalytic converter. This uses a catalyst, and the high temperature in the exhaust pipe, to remove nitrogen monoxide by reacting it with another gas, carbon monoxide.

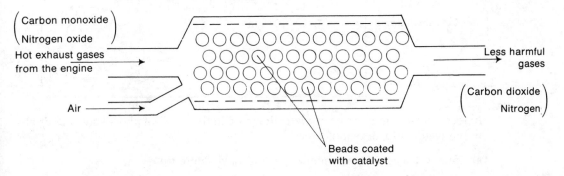

      i)   Explain how carbon monoxide is produced in a motor car engine.

      ii)   What effect does carbon monoxide have on the human body?

      iii) What is a catalyst?

      iv) Which of the two gases released from the converter does no harm to the environment? Explain your answer.

      v)   Suggest a reason for the fact that the catalytic converter can only be used on cars which run on unleaded petrol.

d) Coal-fired power stations can reduce the amount of nitrogen dioxide they produce by burning coal using 'fluidised bed' combustion. This allows the coal to burn efficiently at a lower temperature.

      i)   Explain how this method of burning coal reduces the amount of nitrogen dioxide emitted by the power station.

      ii)   Widespread use of fluidised bed technology would add around 5% to electricity bills. Explain, giving your reasons, whether you think that fluidised bed combustion should be introduced at all coal-fired power stations.

4   Cockshoot Broad is a lake in Norfolk. The map below shows that water flows into Cockshoot Broad from the River Bure. The area is surrounded by farmland that slopes down to the lake.

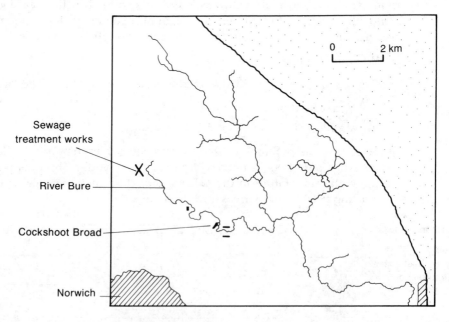

In recent years there has been a large increase in the levels of phosphate and nitrate in the waters of Cockshoot Broad.

a) Suggest where these chemicals could have come from.

b) When high levels of nitrate and phosphate pollute a lake or river, a series of changes takes place in the water, resulting in the death of many fish.

Rewrite the following sentences in the correct order to give a summary of the changes which occur.

Nitrates and phosphates provide essential minerals for the growth of microscopic algae.

Populations of bacteria increase and use up large amounts of oxygen.

Nitrates and phosphates pollute the water.

Oxygen levels in the water drop sharply.

The water becomes green and cloudy as the numbers of algae rise.

Fish die owing to lack of oxygen.

Many algae then die and provide food for decay bacteria.

c) Why is there a build-up of dead organic matter on the bottom of polluted lakes and rivers?

d) In some regions the level of nitrates in drinking water has increased. Why does this give cause for concern?

5 One way to check the amount of pollution in a river is to measure the volume of oxygen dissolved in the water. Another way is to see which sorts of animals are living in it.

This table shows the results of both methods. Use the information in the table to help you answer the questions which follow it.

Amount of pollution	Types of animal present		Volume of oxygen measured (cm^3/l of water)	
	Fish	Others	at 5 °C	at 20 °C
None	Grayling Salmon Trout	Mayfly nymph Stonefly nymph	8	5
Very little	Dace Roach	Freshwater shrimp Snail	6	4
Some	Gudgeon	Bloodworm Water louse	4	3
Lots	None	Rat-tailed maggot Sludge worm	2	1

a) Which *two* animals would you expect to find in water with lots of pollution?

b) Some fish farmers raise trout, which they set free in rivers for anglers to catch.

  i) Explain why these farmers need to be careful about the water supply they use on their fish farms.

  ii) What volume of oxygen, measured in centimetres cubed per litre, would you expect to find in a trout river at 20 °C?

  iii) Describe the pattern linking the temperature of the water and the amount of oxygen in it.

  iv) Suggest and explain what would happen to the number of trout if hot water from a factory was emptied into a trout river and increased the water temperature above 20 °C.

c) In 1974 salmon were caught in the River Thames for the first time in over a hundred years. What does this suggest about the water in the river before 1974?

6 In April 1986, there was an explosion at the Chernobyl nuclear power station in Russia. Radioactivity escaped into the air and was later found to be in rain which fell on Europe.

The map below shows how quickly the radioactive rain spread across Europe.

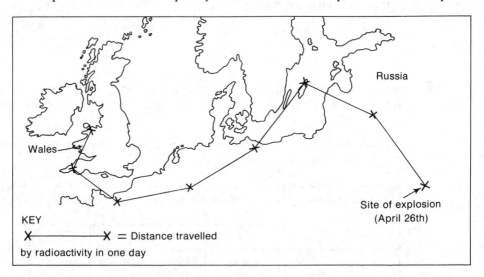

KEY

✗━━━━━━✗ = Distance travelled by radioactivity in one day

a) How many days after the explosion did it take for the radioactive rain to reach Wales?

  The graph on page 30 shows the amount of radioactivity found in the meat of Welsh sheep in the days after the explosion.

b) i) How much radioactivity was found in the meat before the nuclear explosion?

  ii) Suggest reasons for the presence of this radioactivity.

c) i) What was the highest level of radioactivity found in the meat?

  ii) How many days after the explosion did it take to reach this level?

d) When the radioactivity was found in the meat from sheep, the sale of this meat
    was stopped.

    How could radioactive meat harm human cells?

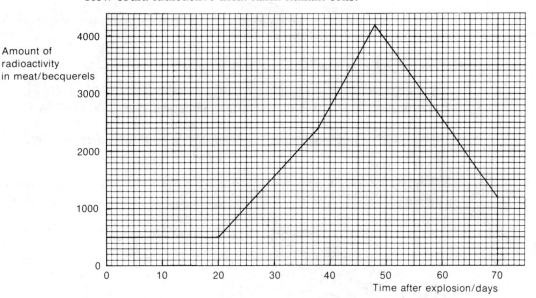

e) Use a table like the one below to list two advantages and two disadvantages of
    generating electricity using nuclear energy.

Advantages of nuclear energy	Disadvantages of nuclear energy

7 Read the passage below and answer the questions which follow.

Ozone is a form of oxygen which has three atoms per molecule. It occurs naturally in
the upper atmosphere, where the ozone layer blocks most of the harmful ultraviolet
radiation from the Sun. At ground level, ozone can be produced as a result of
reactions between pollutants from car exhaust fumes and atmospheric gases. Low-
level ozone is itself a pollutant, which can cause damage to trees and animals. It is a
very reactive gas.

Recently, studies by scientists have shown that, while levels of ozone at ground
level are increasing, the amount of ozone in the upper atmosphere is dropping. One
factor which is thought to be partly responsible for this drop in ozone is the
widespread use of chemicals called CFCs (chlorofluorocarbons). Following release
into the atmosphere, CFCs break down and release chlorine, which reacts with
ozone in the upper atmosphere.

In September 1987, the U.K. government signed the Montreal Protocol, agreeing
to reduce the use of CFCs by 50% by the end of the century. Some scientists believe
that this will not be enough to prevent large-scale damage to life on Earth.

a) What is the molecular formula of
    i)   'normal' oxygen?
    ii) ozone?

b) Give three common uses of CFCs.

c) Suggest one other source of atmospheric chlorine apart from CFCs.

d) Describe one possible consequence for humans of increased exposure to harmful ultraviolet radiation.

e) Suggest reasons why

    i) levels of ozone at ground level are increasing

    ii) ozone produced at ground level does nothing to restore the ozone layer

f) How could *you* personally help to prevent the destruction of the ozone layer?

8 The diagram below supplies information about the sensitivity of some aquatic organisms to the pH of water.

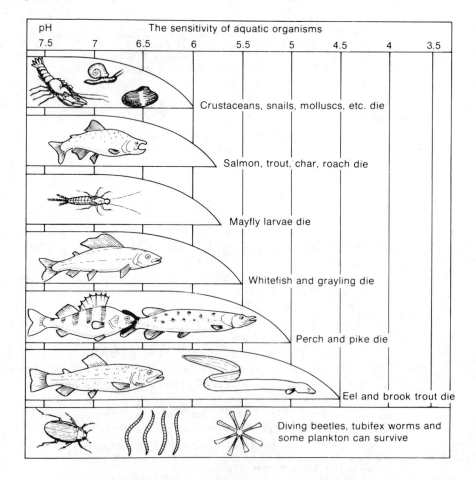

a) i) What is the pH of water below which perch and pike cannot live?

    ii) Which organisms are tolerant of the most acid water?

b) Sulphur dioxide gas can react with other substances in the air producing an acid which lowers the pH of rain.

    i)   Name the acid which is formed.

    ii) Name one other atmospheric pollutant which contributes to acid rain and say where it comes from.

This diagram shows a map of acid rain in western Europe.

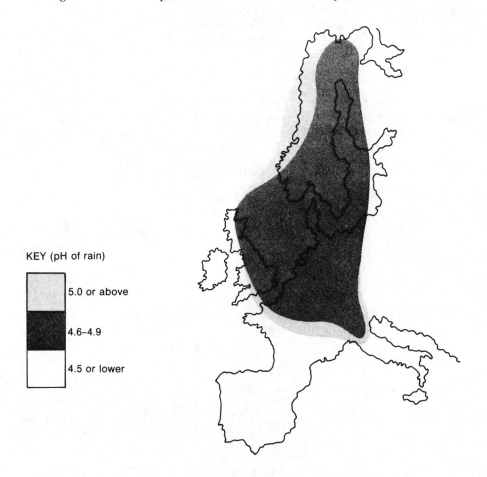

KEY (pH of rain)

5.0 or above

4.6–4.9

4.5 or lower

c) Explain why the pH of the rain falling on Ireland is different from that falling on northern Europe.

d) In Sweden over 9000 lakes no longer contain live fish. Some of the lakes have become 100 times more acidic in the past 50 years.

Explain how this situation may have come about.

e) Most of the sulphur dioxide produced by coal-fired power stations could be removed by absorbing it using 'desulphurisation' equipment. Why is this *not* yet done on a large scale?

f) State *two* other ways in which this form of pollution could be reduced.

9   Write an article for a newspaper which discusses the issues surrounding the destruction of rainforests. You may use the information below to help you.

Rainforests are being destroyed by Man to provide timber and to clear land for ranching and farming, mining and new roads.

About half of the world's rainforest has already gone. An area the size of England, Scotland and Wales goes up in smoke every year.

Tropical hardwoods and the cash crops grown on cleared land provide important income for some poor, developing countries.

Large areas of rainforest in Central America have been cut down to provide grazing for cattle for the American hamburger market. Alternatively it is cleared to grow crops such as soya beans to feed European cattle.

About 200 million tribal people live in the rainforests of the world.

Tropical rainforests soak up water like giant sponges. If trees are cut down in large numbers, the rainwater floods the land. Transpiration from the leaves of the plants is an important part of the water cycle.

Once the trees have gone the rainforest soil will only support the growth of crops or provide grazing for a few years.

A typical patch of rainforest, just 4 miles square, contains as many as 1500 species of flowering plants, up to 750 species of tree, 400 species of bird, 150 kinds of butterfly, 100 different types of reptile and 60 species of amphibian. The numbers of insects are so great that no one has yet been able to count them.

In 1960 four out of every five children who got leukaemia died. Now four out of every five survive thanks to a drug derived from the rosy periwinkle which grows in the rainforests of Madagascar.

10   The burning of fuels produces 14 000 million tonnes of carbon dioxide per year. Carbon dioxide is one of the gases in the atmosphere which allow short wavelength infra-red radiation from the Sun to pass through but which stop some of the long wavelength infra-red radiation from Earth leaving the atmosphere.

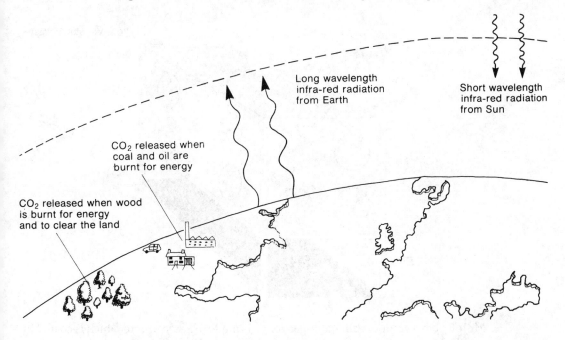

a)   Why is the infra-red radiation re-emitted by the Earth of longer wavelength than that received?

b)   The levels of carbon dioxide in the atmosphere are rising.

   i)   What is the *main* human activity which is contributing to the increase?

   ii)   Suggest and explain one other activity which may also be contributing to this increase.

c)   State and explain what effect the increase in CO_2 levels could have on the

   i)   climate in Britain

   ii)   mean sea level

d)   What effects might the changes you have described in c) have on the lives of people in Britain?

Recycling

1

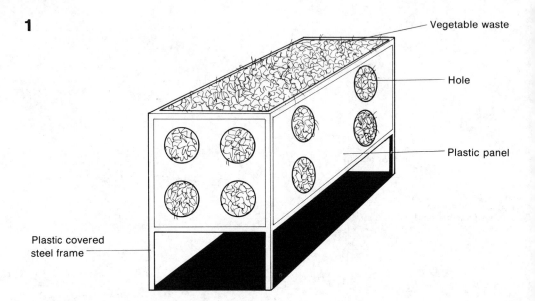

Vegetable waste

Hole

Plastic panel

Plastic covered
steel frame

Mr Jolly has a compost bin in his garden. It is made of a steel frame which is coated in plastic. Plastic panels fit into the sides and bottom of the frame. The plastic panels on the sides have holes in them.

a)   Suggest one reason why

    i)   the frame is made of steel

    ii)   the panels are made of plastic

    iii) the steel frame is coated in plastic

Mr Jolly puts all of his vegetable waste in the compost bin. When the bin is full the waste is left for 12 months. Mr Jolly sometimes waters the compost heap during the summer. After 12 months the vegetable waste has been converted to compost.

b)   Why does Mr Jolly only put vegetable waste in the compost bin and not all of his household waste such as plastic bags, glass bottles and metal cans?

c)   Bacteria break down the vegetable waste into compost. Where do the bacteria come from?

d)   How do these decay bacteria contribute to

    i)   the carbon cycle?

    ii)   the nitrogen cycle?

e)   Why does Mr Jolly need to water the compost bin sometimes during the summer?

f) Sometimes small bits of waste fall out through the holes in the sides of the compost bin. Explain why it would *not* be a good idea for Mr Jolly to block the holes up.

g) Why doesn't Mr Jolly put the vegetable waste straight on to his garden instead of first converting it into compost?

h) i) Much of the refuse collected from houses is buried in the ground. Suggest *two* ways in which this refuse could be put to better use and explain the advantages of your suggestions. Organise your answer in the form of a table:

Use	Advantage

ii) Explain how, in some places, refuse buried in the ground years ago is now providing a useful fuel.

2 a) Why should people be discouraged from using plastic packaging?

b) A supermarket claims that its carrier bags are biodegradable.

Design an experiment to test whether their claim is correct.

3 Carefully read the passage below which is about recycling paper, and answer the questions which follow.

At the moment, about 40% of the trees which are cut down are used for making wood pulp, which is then made into paper. Only 25% of the world's paper is currently recycled, although there is no good technical or economic reason why this recycling rate could not be doubled in the next ten years. Recycling half of the world's paper consumption would meet almost 75% of new paper demand and would prevent millions of hectares of forest from being damaged. Fibre-rich countries like Canada and Sweden are not in the front rank of paper recyclers. Recycling rates are much higher in such fibre-poor countries as Japan, Mexico and the Netherlands. In order to recycle, the waste paper needs to be collected and sorted. Most of the best quality paper for recycling comes from the printing industry and offices. Household waste paper is of a lower quality being mainly newspapers which have a lot of ink on them. The ink must first be removed from the waste paper if high quality recycled paper is to be produced. This is done with caustic soda and hot water. Only about 5–6% is treated in this way because it is quite an expensive process. The remainder is simply pulped with hot water, then screened and washed to remove dirt. Paper recycled in this way is only good enough for making such things as cardboard and paper towels.

a) Why does recycling paper help to conserve forests?

b) Canada and Sweden are described as 'fibre-rich'. What does this mean?

c) Why do you think 'fibre-poor' countries recycle more paper?

d) Where does the best quality paper for recycling come from?

e) i) How is waste paper treated to remove ink?

    ii) Why is only a small percentage of paper to be recycled treated in this way?

f) Suggest ways in which people could be encouraged to save waste for recycling.

4 a) Copy these sentences about the **carbon cycle**. Choose words from the following list and fill in the gaps. (The words may be used more than once.)

> plants   decay   respiration   animals   photosynthesis
> combustion   carbon dioxide

i) _____ use carbon dioxide and water to make sugars by the process of _____.

ii) _____ and _____ break down sugars into carbon dioxide and water by the process of _____.

iii) When animals and plants die, their bodies _____.

iv) During the process of decay, microbes return _____ to the atmosphere.

v) Carbon dioxide is removed from the air by the process of _____ and put back into it by the processes of _____ and _____.

vi) When fossil fuels are burnt, carbon dioxide is returned to the atmosphere. This process is called _____.

b) Name *two* fossil fuels. How are they formed?

c) Draw a diagram to show how the processes of **photosynthesis, respiration, combustion** and **decay** are involved in the carbon cycle.

5 The bacteria involved in the **nitrogen cycle** are:

decay bacteria   **nitrifying bacteria**   **nitrogen-fixing bacteria**
denitrifying bacteria

a) Copy the following diagram, which summarises the nitrogen cycle, and in the boxes write the names of the bacteria active at each stage.

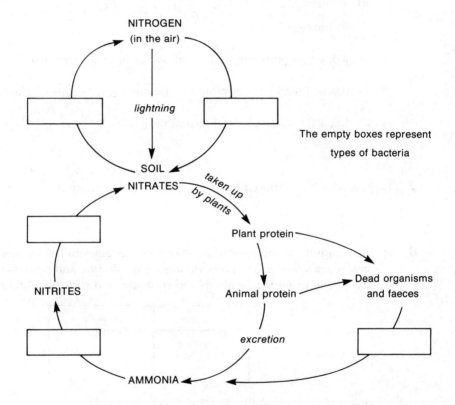

b) In the nitrogen cycle, which of the bacteria are helpful and which are unhelpful?

6 Answer these questions about the **nitrogen cycle**:

a) Why is nitrogen essential for life?

b) How do

    i)   plants

    ii) animals

  obtain nitrogen?

c) Why does the nitrogen cycle work better in well aerated soil?

d) Why is soil made more fertile by growing peans, beans or clover?

e) During a flood the soil will lose nitrates. Why?

7 Explain why it is important to recycle elements in nature.

8 a) Respiration and photosynthesis are two processes in the carbon cycle. Listed below are seven pairs of descriptions of respiration and photosynthesis. Draw up a table using the headings shown below and sort them into two groups:

Respiration	Photosynthesis

    i)   occurs in all cells/occurs in green plant cells

    ii)   energy is released/energy is stored

    iii) produces carbon dioxide/produces oxygen

    iv) produces food/produces water

    v)   uses oxygen/uses carbon dioxide

    vi) uses water/uses food

    vii) occurs only in the light/occurs all the time

b) The air around us contains oxygen and carbon dioxide in amounts that do not vary very much. Using the information from the correctly completed table above, explain why this is so.